Praise for *Woma*

"What and who is a 'witch'? What if [...]
human psyche actively suppressed by western (an[...]
tures for millennia — resources that are feminine, sacred, and utterly
natural at their roots? What if these resources are essential for the
wholeness of *all* humans and for all life-enhancing cultural transformation, especially at this time of global unrest? In this engaging, bold,
and intimate book, Danielle Dulsky provides keys to unlock ancient
portals behind which perilous and pivotal treasures await."

— **BILL PLOTKIN**, author of *Soulcraft: Crossing into the Mysteries of
Nature and Psyche* and *Wild Mind: A Field Guide to the Human Psyche*

"With all that modern women are facing — from political activism to
personal growth to motherhood — it's all too easy for us to lose our
inner spark. More than ever, we need to reclaim the lost art of what
Danielle Dulsky calls 'wild woman spirituality' by calling forth the archetype of the witch. In *Woman Most Wild*, Dulsky shows us how to
do just this, by schooling us in the art of what she calls 'She-Magick.'
Rich with rituals, stories, and invocations, *Woman Most Wild* offers
every woman a whimsical handbook to reclaiming the lost art of feminine magic — medicine that our world sorely needs."

— **SARA AVANT STOVER**, author of *The Way of the Happy Woman*
and *The Book of SHE*

"Just as other oppressed people have reclaimed the very words meant to
oppress them, Danielle Dulsky is reclaiming perhaps the most powerful word used against women throughout history. The patriarchy has
used this word to shame and silence women — and even to burn them
at the stake. The word is *witch*. And Dulsky has dared to reclaim it in
this deeply alchemical and passionate book. Not only does she brave
the word but she also restores the rich, embodied meanings and uses it
inspires. Dulsky speaks from deep in her soul to deep in our souls. She
speaks to a longing born of the feminine's spiritual starvation and offers
a fierce and sensual reclamation of the wild women we were born to be."

— **DEBORAH KAMPMEIER**, Full Moon Films,
writer and director of *Hounddog*, *Virgin*, and *SPLiT*

Woman Most Wild

Woman Most Wild

Three Keys to Liberating the Witch Within

DANIELLE DULSKY

New World Library
Novato, California

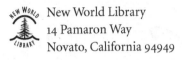 New World Library
14 Pamaron Way
Novato, California 94949

Text design by Tracy Cunningham

Library of Congress Cataloging-in-Publication Data
Names: Dulsky, Danielle, [date]–author.
Title: Woman most wild : three keys to liberating the witch within / Danielle Dulsky.
Description: Novato, CA : New World Library, 2017. | Includes bibliographical references and index.
Identifiers: LCCN 2016056192 (print) | LCCN 2017011028 (ebook) | ISBN 9781608684663 (alk. paper) | ISBN 9781608684670 (Ebook)
Subjects: LCSH: Wicca. | Witchcraft.
Classification: LCC BP605.W53 D85 2017 (print) | LCC BP605.W53 (ebook) | DDC 220.8/13343—dc23
LC record available at https://lccn.loc.gov/2016056192

First printing, May 2017
ISBN 978-1-60868-466-3
Ebook ISBN 978-1-60868-467-0
Printed in Canada on 100% postconsumer-waste recycled paper

 New World Library is proud to be a Gold Certified Environmentally Responsible Publisher. Publisher certification awarded by Green Press Initiative. www.greenpressinitiative.org

10   9   8   7   6   5   4   3

To my grandmother, Grace,
for growing my Maiden's roots strong.

To my men, Bodhi, Sage, and Ryan,
for keeping my Mother's heart whole.

To my Council of Five
for keeping my Wise Woman's spirit wild.

✦— This Truth

Snuff out the candles! Make the room dark!
I'll cradle you close, star-shaped child.
Inside your heart's ripe, red center — a spark!
When I speak of Her rhythm, this Woman Most Wild.

She lives in a hut made of soft guts and hard bones,
She crawls out of your mouth while you sleep.
In the forest, the desert, She sets up Her stones
'Fore bare-breasted swimming in the salty blue deep.

When She comes back to your body, Her hearth and Her home,
She's tired, and filthy, and fed.
She hopes that you'll notice the sand, water, and loam
She's painted all over your bed.

Peel off her hard mask, the woman so mild,
And drink of the succulent moon.
You, my sweet one, are the Woman Most Wild.
You'll swallow this truth whole and soon.

*C*ontents

---❧---

Introduction

—⚮—

$\mathcal{M}$y love, in these pages I will speak to you as my Sister, as if we were sipping rosehip tea and sharing stories of how we first found our magick so long ago, deep within the wild place. I will tell you of your part in the collective feminine awakening, and I will honor you as a high-level Priestess. I am neither above you nor below you; we sit at the same table. I, too, have felt the heart-centered ignition of a soul well nourished, and you already know what I am about to tell you. Woman, you have a Witch's soul buried deep within your busy psychic terrain, and that part of you yearns to live in alignment with the rhythms of nature, to mark transitions with ritual, and to be healed with the medicine of sisterhood. These are the keys to your Witch's liberation, and they are already yours. You, my Sister-Witch, already know of your birthright as a woman of this wild world, but I am calling on you to remember. You already know, but now, right this minute, I ask you to open your eyes wide to the Mystery and surrender to your inner alchemical wildness that is Witch.

A communal subterranean yearning for wild woman spirituality is drumming underneath our feet, and this longing has been born of the feminine's spiritual starvation. Notably and understandably dissatisfied are we with our apparent limited options for divine connection. Facing a spiritual void, we are pushed too quickly toward prepackaged religious meals, sold to us in myriad forms. Left with famished souls, we dismiss any hope of finding true spiritual autonomy and commit to a path far more limiting than what we deserve. Wild One, we deserve it *all*. As women, we are the embodiment of the feminine divine and the very essence of the cosmic dance. Our spirits burn with star-stuff, and we were born to be spiritually empowered.

YOUR WILD HOMECOMING

I see you now, a woman whole in her soul, body, mind, and spirit. Crouching in the shadows of the triple-locked broom closet you are. You may feel it is not worth the trouble to stand firm on your muddy bare feet and use those three keys you hold in your left hand. You may fear condemnation. You may want so much to be in control when you have a bone-deep knowing that your most authentic self is limitless, untamed, and ancient. In these pages I will show you how to open the door that keeps your spirituality so neatly and apologetically contained. Unlock this closet carved with the claw marks of your inner Witch, and liberate Her soul, and I will call you out as a Woman Most Wild. Hear me when I tell you there is nothing to fear, and take these words to heart: Opening that door will bring you to the sweetest homecoming you have ever known.

Remember the innocence with which you used to welcome the first warm morning in spring. You became a medium for the sheer electricity of new life. You were fed by the rising gush of Gaia's green juices as they groundswelled under your grass-stained knees. Sister, you, so raw and awake, knew in your blood what it meant to be a wild Witch long before you were a grown woman. In the heat of summer, your Maiden's intuition told you to lie in the grass and be infused with sensual solar power, and you listened. When the leaves began to drop so ceremoniously from their branches in autumn, you relished the death ritual with all that you were, knowing you would soon rest in your fire-lit nest as the first winter's snow coated the outside world. You were Witch as a young girl, my love, and you are Witch still.

Pause now. Close your eyes. Sink into the softness of your perfect body. Sift through your memories, recollections of a time that may seem too far-gone to be real, and affirm who you are: *I am a Witch.* In this moment, you are on the edge of reclaiming your wild woman's soul as part of your identity. I, as your sister, hold that you are harboring an untamed, unseen creatrix who, when unleashed, will offer you the truest, most sacred, most needed nourishment to those raw parts of yourself that are so thirsty for greater meaning and deeper authenticity.

MY PROMISE TO YOU

You need not be fully comfortable with naming yourself Witch. It only makes sense, after thousands of years of society's sharp blade stabbing deep into women's divine integrity, for the word *Witch* to provoke an automatic belly tightening. It was not so long ago when any number of practices aligning your feminine soul with the natural world would have led to legal, if not fatal, ramifications. You know this, and such a deep knowing is as inherent to your blood as iron. Our soul-wound still bleeds, and it runs bright red for the loss of feminine spirituality. While I wholeheartedly believe that many religious paths need not be incompatible with the ways of the Witch, there are those who will tell you differently. I make a promise to you now, my Sister, and tell you that the way of the Witch is entirely your own.

I promise that I will not argue for you to relinquish any part of your belief system you hold as true. I vow to continually affirm your spiritual autonomy. You are who you say you are, and there is no Priestess so enlightened she has the right to rob you of the names you have given yourself. Harvesting your Witch's soul means making good and personally relevant use of what I call the three keys to the broom closet.

These are your own physical, emotional, and spiritual rhythms as they intimately converse with those of the natural world; your personal practices of magick and ritual; and, most important, your sacred circle of other wild women. In these pages I will offer you spicy tastes and vibrant visions of Witchcraft as a way of life. I will ask you to listen, and listen closely, for heart-whispers and guttural howls from deep within your feminine psyche. Listen as your Witch consciousness awakens and speaks in Her own voice, and know that the call of the wild never sounds the same to any two sets of ears.

I call you out as a Witch but offer you no religion. Instead, what I offer you in these pages are glimpses of how your soft and perfect being may be infused with the marrow of ritual, magick, and circle-craft. My purpose is not to gift you with an entirely new way of living but to offer clarity on an alternative way of *being* in this world. You have the bright eyes of a Woman Most Wild, my Sister, and I will show you how to use those soul-windows to see the majestic beauty in all things but especially in your holy self. In these pages I will invite you to insert those three keys into their magickal locks and set your Witch's soul irrevocably free.

Know the Witch as a wise presence that is fiercely feminine. Know the Witch as a wild woman who has embraced nature's spiral dance. Know her as a keen-eared, sharp-sighted healer who has her own way of conversing with the world. Now, know yourself as Her. To be a Witch is to be a woman of the Earth. To be a Witch is to see the mystical in the mundane, bright beauty in the fertile darkness, and, most salient, the sheer merit of being unapologetically and fearlessly *you*. You are poised to experience the liberation of unbridled spirituality, and I am honored, just for a time, to walk with you on your path.

The very foundation of my sacred work is a hearty formidable bridge between the traditional women's circle and the Witches' coven. You, my Sister-Witch, crave both the warm womb-space of a women's circle and the electric magick of coven work. *Coven* is a very broad term for a group of men and women who practice many variations of paganism, both religious and nonreligious. Traditional covens have nourished the spiritual thirst of many men and women throughout the global community, as has Wicca, the diverse religion firmly grounded in the Craft. Alternatively, Witchcraft is a flexible, liberating, and non-religious practice that serves as the undiluted, fully adaptable essence of feminine spirituality.

Witchcraft is an inclusive practice that demands nothing of you, and there is no test you must pass before you can call yourself a Witch. Know this, my love: Any spiritual path that renders you choiceless is not truly a feminist path, and the spiritual poverty affecting many women comes largely from our long-standing exclusion from positions of power in patriarchal religion. The very nature of spirituality is connection and union, with the divisive dogmas of many religions not only precluding access for women and members of the LGBTQ+ community but also misaligning with the very necessary role of spirituality in a human life.

Deeply rooted and malicious weeds strangle many seemingly feminist traditions, and rigidly organized Witchcraft is no exception to this unfortunate, often unnoticed reality; hierarchy, greed, control, and ego-born power will compromise the best-intended and most compassionate spiritual paths. The remedy to the pervasive exclusion of authentic equality within spiritual communities is to infuse all facets of the organization with the freedom of choice, inclusion, and nonhierarchal structures. Women have been uniquely robbed of their spiritual power, and the reclamation of wild spirituality, that is, practices and understandings that acknowledge the untamed, holy, and spiraling qualities of the natural world as living within all beings, is paramount to pan-gender equality.

For the Wild Good of Women, for the Wild Good of All

I wrote these pages for the woman who has sensed her inner Wild One poking at her ribs but has kept her contained, unsure of how to negotiate her liberation. My words are also for the seasoned Witch seeking some literary nourishment, the Witch's friend hoping to understand her Soul-Sister better, and anyone who has sensed a spiritual void born from the loss of the divine feminine. While this book is primarily for those who identify as women, your wild spirituality does not require a physical womb; it only asks you to honor the fusion of your body and psyche to your feminine spirit. Though ritual is a vital and load-bearing pillar in the Witch's house, this book is much more of a three-part ode to your inborn wild wisdom than a how-to manual for conducting rituals and crafting spells. A wealth of books is available to those seeking such resources, and I would urge you to begin by considering the foundations I offer here. We are both Priestesses on our own paths, but in these pages, my bare feet will step in time with yours.

Just as salient, let me say that while I believe the reclamation of Witchcraft is an act of women's liberation, an affirmation of our feminine birthright in a world where we have been historically subjugated, it is much more a cultivation of feminine spirituality that is positively and fiercely pan-gender. The global community has been collectively orphaned by the loss of the sacred feminine, and wild woman spirituality is, and indeed will be, instrumental in reviving Her. All human beings, independent of a dominant gender orientation, embody qualities of the masculine and feminine, and the whole of humanity has suffered from the aggressions of the immature and nongenerative masculine. I have titled this book *Woman Most Wild* not to isolate anyone who does not identify as a woman but to empower toward freedom the wild woman archetype within the global collective.

Here I want to say that the rejection of transgender women from traditional women's circles has been an unfortunate, underhanded instrument of oppression labeled as feminism. Those who resonate with the wild woman archetype have an inner value system that is fiercely inclusive, and the feminine is not defined by biology. The Wild Mother opens her arms to all of us, and we must take great care to honor all her children, letting our circles be a microcosm of the world we want to live in.

Uncaging the wild woman means rallying against oppression, standing up for those who are sociopolitically and socioeconomically precluded from standing on their own, and honoring the beauteously untamable and miraculously unruined spirit within us all. We are all of the Earth, and it is wild. Your spiritual liberation is an act of social justice. The presentation of the twisted-nosed Crone-Witch in fairy tales as the poisoner of children is an instrument of feminine suppression that very much parallels the denigration of the environment. The Earth is feminine, and the continual threats to Her autonomy have coincided directly and historically with the oppression of women. By robbing the mythical Witch of her beauteous humanity and rendering her a malicious presence, the tales of our childhood rendered her socially powerless. The Witch is a holy healer who attunes Herself with the drumbeat of nature. She has heard the trees crying, and She will no longer allow herself to remain in the shadows while the voiceless are ignored. Her time has come, and She is beckoning for you to come wander with Her.

A Note for the Urban Witch

Wild woman spirituality ignites a soul-deep kinship with nature, and this is true whether you live miles from your closest neighbor or within a densely populated city. As a wholly inclusive practice, the ways of the Witch are many and varied. This Craft excludes no one, and the urban Witch is uniquely positioned to have greater access to certain resources, the greatest of which is other like-minded wild women and existing circles. Most of the nature-based rituals described in this book can be adapted for those without access to open and green spaces. If you live in a place without safe access to open and green spaces, I recommend dedicating a space in your home to your Holy Wild; ideally, this is a place where sacred relics, plants, or symbols of the natural world can remind you that you are forever held by the Earth and Her elements. This is your Wild Home within your home, your sanctuary. Moreover, if you live in an urban setting, consider the ways in which the built structures frame the wild world rather than suppress it. Acknowledge the magick of the city as a sacred circle in its own right in which high-energy vibrations abound, human connections are readily forged, and the pulse of Mother Earth beats beneath it all.

READ WILDLY

Your spiritual liberation comes from a Craft that ebbs and flows over rough ground, carving out deep trenches in places where you crave it most often, spilling over its banks in times of loss or fierce need, and finding new rivulets when the high-edged ego begins to crumble to the holy ground. Let all parts of you feed this wild river, especially the exotic mud of your sensuality and the many-colored waters of your creativity. The Witch is being re-wilded through the reclamation of the fem-force, or Shakti, and She is being re-wilded through you.

Just like your spiritual path, each part of this book is intended to be unpacked in your own way and in your own time. Some chapters you may liken to a thick, hot, ceremonial cacao drink; they are not to be consumed quickly or absentmindedly, and the words may make your heart beat faster and take time to digest. Other chapters may slide down your gullet like so much rosewater, clean and familiar. The integration of any new spiritual practice should curdle your blood just a bit, for it threatens the natural human ego's desire to already know everything about its world. Know that every word of this text has been written from my Witch's soul to yours, with the feminine divine's voice echoing at my heart center with all the grace of our grandmothers. I invite you now to read wildly, to loosen your grip on the three keys of rhythm, ritual, and circle-craft, and to begin planning the festival of your sacred homecoming. I will hang the banners for you, my love, and I will invite every Wolf-Woman I know to your Witch's debutante ball.

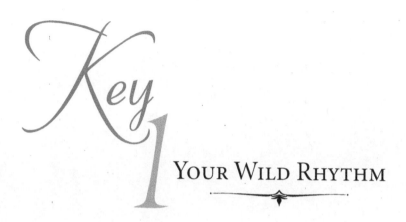

Key 1

YOUR WILD RHYTHM

✦ Invocation

I made the holiest vows in utter silence,

Trusting that an ancient version of myself was listening,

Knowing that in a time long gone, I was being heard.

My heart-voice echoed through the Mother oaks,

And this wounded woman from a world at war learned
who she was

Only by listening to her own voice on a warm wind.

The ebbs and flows of the great Earth's natural cycles live within you, Witch. Know the wild feminine as circular, and concerned above all else with the interconnectedness of all things. That logical left brain of yours wants to separate, fragment, and linearize all that you perceive, but your generative, intuitive right brain knows a deeper truth. In your cells you know that this world lives in you as much as you live in *it*. I call this magickal life for which you are destined your spiritual integrity, but in truth it is your physical, mental, and soulful integrity as well. The rhythms of nature are the rhythms of your energetic womb, the cycles of your emotions and creative work, and the continual, spiraling understanding that divinity exists in it all, forever and always. The recollection of your embodied cycles is the key to the broom closet's first lock; without this, your Witch consciousness remains dormant.

The intentional embodiment of your wild rhythm is integral to your spirituality because it grounds you firmly in this world; it creates opportunity for continual affirmation of your sexuality and creativity as hallmarks of your very nature. There is no great chasm between your enduring spirit and your holy, sensual self. The rhythms of the wild world are proof of your holistic being. Your sex and your spirit were forced into a divorce long ago, but now, *now* let these two parts of you

be reunited under red satin sheets. The first pillar of wild woman spirituality is the marriage between the Witch's whole being — that is, her soul, body, mind, and spirit — and the cycles of the world around her. You are not merely in the world, my love; you are *of* the world.

When a woman's life becomes isolated from the cycles of nature's magick, she not only experiences a starvation of soul and spirit; she begins to question her sanity. The psyches and bodies of women are meant to wax and wane, swelling and thinning out with much majestic variability. The feminine is neither even-keeled nor easily predicted. We are changeable creatures. We women experience spiritual winters during which there is a divinely fallowed time when we care not for prayer or ritual. So, too, a woman experiences these sacred voids in terms of love and relationship, body and health, creative work, and every aspect of her way of being in the world. When compared directly and unknowingly to a high-fire inner summer, when deep, purposeful, and fertile transformation is being birthed over and over again, these inner winters can weigh heavily on a woman. She sinks low into a depression made far worse by a rejection of this time's validity as a dark-moon psychic state during which a woman craves solitude and emptiness.

The rhythms of the Holy Wild give us permission to have our own cyclical nature; we need only frame these highs and lows as part of our bodily and psychic home. We are the living feminine, Sister, and we have a cosmically sanctioned right to check in and check out in accordance with our inner resources. Our energetic wells can only source so much work, so much play, so much nurturing, and so much devotion before they become depleted. Consider the solar and lunar cycles as more predictable metaphors for your own rhythms. We are not meant to be constantly turned on, and the world needs our darkness as much as it needs our light.

From the time we are girls we learn to shut down our natural and intermittent inclination to run into the dark void of nothingness. Idle hands, after all, are the devil's playthings. Who knows what the wild child might do if her imagination were left unbridled? The technologies of woman taming are as old as dirt, my love, and the most sinister of these has been the strategic condemnation of the Still Woman. Remember that when I say "wild," I do not mean out of control; rather, I refer to the freedom of both stillness and doing, a sacred liberation that was slowly taken from us when we were young. The wild is your human way of relating to the life-force that is beyond human but wholly natural.

Little girls are kept wild when their caregivers affirm their right, and affirm it often, to be of the world. A good deal of preparation for the battle of adolescence is necessary in order for children of all genders to psychologically survive the woundings that will inevitably occur. Particularly for those who do not neatly match our culture's presented image of normalcy, the survival skills required are immense, with the suppression of the wild a common response to the threat of abandonment. During adolescence, we fear looking or acting out of alignment with what our peers have deemed acceptable. We conform in order to belong, in order to keep from being left behind, with every act of perceived rejection driving the wild self deeper into the shadows of our psyche.

It is beyond terrifying, I know, to crack wide open the shell that has been layered so thickly around us by so many years of snickers, eye rolls, turned backs, insults, and punishments. Hear me when I tell you that you are not who they say you are, and the greatest gift you can give to the global community is to be fiercely authentic. Unlearn the mechanisms of control that keep you believing that you must keep going no matter how loud your heart-voice is screaming for rest. Reclaim your wild rhythm, and awaken your Witch consciousness; she is sleeping, small body curled with the petrification that comes of allowing ourselves only small movements these past years. Wake her now. Wake her up, and let her show you the way home.

I see you now, my Sister-Witch, ear pressed against the door, hearing the call of your wild nature like a gut-born drumbeat. The ping-pat of raindrops, the mother wolf's howl, the songs of birds you cannot name: All these things have been nested in your soul since you were a young girl. Remember now. Remember the nourishment of nature-aligned rhythm, and insert that ancient, rusted key into the lock.

Remember the electric buzz you felt in your heart when gazing upward at the maternal full moon. Turn the key, letting it groan like the ancient iron it is. Hear the sound of your inner Witch waking up with a soft, sultry yawn bellowed from beneath your ribs. Embodying the rhythms of this strong Earth is your first act of liberation, and it is the most fundamental, central pillar of wild woman spirituality. Once you have acknowledged the organic power of the world around you as kith and kin to that which lies within you, once *that* is done, there will be no turning back.

Chapter 1

The Holy Moon
and Your Witch Consciousness

———————◆———————

*E*very living aspect of our natural world embodies the masculine and the feminine, including you, my Sister-Witch. The philosophy of Tantra teaches us that both the masculine and feminine energies are divine, with the feminine being immanent within all things. The sun and moon are the celestial reflections of these two polarities, with the sun as the pulsating, ever-burning masculine and the moon as the mysterious, ever-spiraling, and oh-so-cool feminine. By day the sun feeds our hunger for action and clear vision. By night the moon quenches our thirst for intuitive foresight and shortly lived cycles of birth, fullness, and emptiness. Both the solar and lunar rhythms of this world are cyclical, and we, as human beings, are fed by each of these Earth-sustaining bodies; the masculine is our spicy sustenance, and the feminine is our chill mineral water. We eat of the sun and drink of the moon; both nourish our bones and our blood.

In this chapter I will share with you the clean essence of the moon's cycles as they live within your wild nature, but the most critical piece of information is this: Just as the moon is an alchemical celestial body that, to our Earthly perspective, is always in a state of change, so, too, is the Witch a creature of ever-spiraling transformation. You have no *one* way to be, and this chapter offers you glimpses of a woman's cyclical nature. You may read a certain passage and wonder if the image I present of a woman weeping in the dark could possibly be lived out by the same woman who was dancing by a fire in the woods on previous pages; I say *yes*. By all that is blessed and holy, *yes*. We take for granted the ways of the moon, but we understand the symbiotic relationship between the bright fullness of fruition and the nail-thin silver sliver of near-nothingness as a perfect metaphor for how changeable we are. To be in flux is the feminine's nature, and such is the way of lunar life. You must give yourself permission to change constantly, every sleep a restful sort of moonlit labor during which you give birth to a new version of yourself just as the sun rises.

Your Witch consciousness is very much bound to the rhythm of Mother Moon. Intuitively, you have known the promise of the waxing lunar cycle, like a well-built wood stack crackling just after the kindling is lit. The height of the flames, like so much unbridled energy and surging heat, you have known as the full moon essence, with the dying fire akin to the waning lunar cycle. After the fire has completely fizzled and there is naught but smoking ash, you are in dark moon time. Each of these four phases is framed within the enduring boundaries of the twenty-nine-day period, and each of these four phases is mirrored within your energetic womb.

Your age matters not. These moon beats live inside you regardless of your stage of life or status in the world, as do the archetypes of the sensual Maiden, creative Mother, and wise Crone. Know these time-worn concepts of the Triple Goddess nature not as successive life phases, for such predictability is the stuff of linear time. You can liken your inner Maiden to your rawest sexuality and fluid emotionality, your inner Mother to generative work and high-fire creativity, and your inner Crone to your deep intuitive, receptive nature. Even a young girl embodies Crone, just as a wise elder holds much sensuality. Women are the spiral dance, and our time does not move in straight lines.

Living in alignment with lunar changes will serve you so much more than living in accordance with any calendar. Your soul will be nourished every time you invoke the essence of a lunar phase, harnessing the warrior-woman energy of a new moon, the sheer, electric force of a full moon, the release and acceptance that comes with the waning phase, and the oh-so-potent thick void of a dark moon. These rhythms are already internalized within you, Woman. You need only acknowledge them as part of your truest self, allow them to inform your movements through the world, and learn what they have to teach you.

Before you continue reading this chapter, take a moment to recall your childhood memories of the moon. Remember the intrigue of that changeable gray-white celestial body with the mystery-laden face and soft blue halo. Remember the moon before you learned to take it for granted. Just in this moment, be that restless little girl again who cannot sleep and looks longingly out her window, wondering how she knows this maternal light so intimately.

DRINKING MOON MILK: A LUNAR MEDITATION

As you read this now, flip your palms skyward and tilt your head back just a bit. Lift your gaze, and sense the energy around you. Visualize the perfect moon above you, regardless of whether you know its current phase. Sense the celestial body's steady path around the Earth, and know this moon as the essence of the primal, ancient feminine. Envision the lunar energy field as vibrating with a soft diamond-white glow and, now, with every inhale, pull the moon's essence into you. Down, down, down the moonlight descends, entering your third-eye center, the intuitive space between and above your brows, with every inhale. As you exhale, let this diamond-light get more vibrant. Inhaling, draw the moon essence deep into your being, slowly being filled with these vibrations all the way down to your roots. Exhaling as the moon milk fills your sweet, soft body, let the brilliant energy glow brighter, and brighter, and brighter still. Inhaling and exhaling. Breathing in the moon and letting the moon breathe you.

Drink in this moon milk with all that you are. Surrender to lunar replenishment. You glow now with Goddess light, with all the divinity of the cosmos. Woman, what an amazing beauty you are! Let the lunar light nourish every cell, bone, muscle, and organ in your body. Let Her burn away your insecurities, your guilt, your shame, your fears. Just for now, just in this very moment, let the moon have its way with you.

Swallow this moon milk and feel your inner Witch revel inside your ribs. You are bringing the juice back into her veins now, and she tells you this: *There you are, Woman! I have been waiting for so long! Let me show you the Old Ways. I will remind you of sacred sensuality and the soul-food of a night spent wild. I will deepen every experience with my womb-wise intelligence, and I will tell you of your power. Remember who you are, a Woman Most Wild, a Witch liberated, and the Goddess embodied. Stay fed and full, my Sister, for this is only the beginning.* Your inner Witch is wide awake now. Let's learn of your sacred rhythms and make her dance!

A woman craves practical knowledge of her soulful cycles, for she intuitively understands that she will not open her eyes tomorrow morning as the same woman she was today. Many of our bumpiest scars stem from our neglect of our cyclical nature; such patterning, when combined with the pervasive social rejection of our changeable nature, has dug a deep chasm into our self-awareness. Clarissa Pinkola Estés, in her treatise on the wild woman archetype, *Women Who Run with the Wolves*, emphasizes the importance of women's cycles, arguing against the notion of women's entire lives being compartmentalized into three seasons of girl, woman, and elder: "We cannot allow ourselves to sleepwalk wrapped in this flimsy and unobservant fabrication, for it causes women to deviate from their natural and soulful cycles." A bone-deep fear of change runs rampant in our patriarchal society, dear Sister, and you may have noticed even those who truly love you act out a desire to keep you static. Honor your cycles, knowing they are far more complex than those described here. Accept your righteously alchemical nature.

Drink the lunar nectar, and reclaim your nature as a mother-loving shape-shifter, and hear me when I tell you that you were born to be ever-changing.

LET THE WITCH SPEAK!
Hearing Her Womb-Voice under the Moon

The Witch thinks, speaks, and prays with Her whole body. Sense the location of your thoughts now, my love. Do they live just at the crown of your head? Perhaps a few inches lower? Feel where your thinking mind is centered, and now begin to pull your thinking mind down to your third eye, that space of reception where your most authentic vision lives, and then lower to your throat center. Here is the place of truth, story, and voice. Pull your thinking mind down even deeper to your heart, where you will sense the energy of compassion and gratitude, then even farther to your solar plexus, where your very ego and identity reside, surrounded by the fire of your will and self-esteem. Finally, let your thinking mind drop down to your sacral center, between your hip bones. Here you are at the source of your womb-wisdom and your Witch voice.

Ask of your sacral center only one question now, and let it be this: What do I need to know right at this moment, under this moon? Let the answer bubble up from that sacred, sacral space and climb through your energy centers to your throat. The voice that whispers from your lips now is your womb-voice. Even if you do not have a physical uterus, your energetic wise womb remains and has much to say. Do not let this womb-voice startle you, Woman, for it may say things that both shock and inspire. Can you hear the tone in which your womb-voice is speaking? Can you hear it echo from your pelvic bowl as if the Goddess herself were howling from inside an ancient cave temple? Let her speak. Give her permission — not that she needs it — to tell you of your wild worth.

Learning to hear this holy voice, your truest voice, is a vital skill that will serve you well, my love; it is the very technology of feminine guidance. Once your inner Witch knows you are listening, she will speak louder and more often. She will offer you guidance when you need it, though not necessarily when you are looking for it, and she will teach you her language. Know that she may not speak in words you know; she may speak through energetic pulses in your body, sudden glimpses of images in your wild psyche, or subtle feelings that could easily be ignored, were you less still and aware. Find just enough presence every night to hone the ways of deep listening, trusting this practice is part of your holy birthright and devoting a small part of yourself to hearing your inner voices as the moon waxes and wanes.

THE NEW MOON'S SPARK
Your Lunar Dawn

The new moon bubbles in your blood as if your very body were a cauldron of skin-framed, magickal brew. The earliest days of the new moon phase are marked by a subtle sense that your creativity and sensuality have been somehow heightened. An awareness of a slow build both within and outside you can render even the wisest woman anxious and hypervigilant; being aware of this lunar phase is therefore vital to your identity as a creatrix. Artist you are, Woman, regardless of whether you are birthing new life in your womb, carefully shaping a bit of clay, cooking up some hearty soup, or decorating your hearth for a holiday. All this, and every infinitesimal act on the creative spectrum, is the hallmark of new moon fire.

The subtle and blatant bursts of creativity you feel as the moon waxes are a sort of internal spring, if we were to liken this lunar energy to a solar season. New growth stirs underground in late winter and erupts from Gaia's mud at the vernal equinox. The new moon is a mini-spring every month, with the warrior-woman energy writhing within you like so many red fire serpents. Honor this time as an energetic growth period. Do not cage your inner warrior, for she needs to be set loose now and then.

I hear you, my Sister, when you say desire can seem unladylike. I understand you when you say that you are no warrior, but I am telling you that this lunar dawn is a fertile time for starting all things new. As the moon waxes, you may become so full with creative energy, your prana Shakti, that you feel you may well explode like a violent volcano. Be the Maiden Goddess at this time and honor your sensuality by feeling, tasting, smelling, hearing, and seeing everything. Your wild woman spirit is inextricably bound to your sacred sexuality, and the new moon holds the very essence of well-purposed passion.

Painting the Wild New Moon: A Creative Dive

Gather these materials, Woman: a blank canvas and bright paint mixed from nontoxic natural elements. Put on no music; hear the night. Drink no wine; taste the iron of passion's fire. Burn no sacred herbs; smell the rawness of your unwashed artist's passion. This void of a canvas calls you to dive deeply into the inferno of the creatrix. Do it now!

Muster your creative mania and slather the vibrant thick color on your fingers. Pull, poke, and pinken that canvas in motions that no artist has ever made before. This is your masterpiece. Do not overthink it. Just paint as if you were the Goddess coloring the world for the first time. Every line, however unbeauteous seeming, is pure in its right to be there. Stomp and spit on the thing if it feels right, my love. You can do no wrong here, and those hands of yours know exactly how to move. Forget the outcome, though it may hang on your walls as a beacon of your rawest and most unbridled creativity. For now, there is nothing except you and this work. Paint yourself to life and then to death, and do it over and over again.

The new moon calls you to break down barriers and fight your way, sword drawn, through crowds of naysayers, even if these obstacles exist only in the confines of your psyche. If you find yourself assessing or judging your work, stop painting and recenter. Let yourself be fed by the waxing lunar energy until you can consume no more, and then collapse onto the floor with a tired, paint-splattered body and an invigorated soul. You have colored the wild new moon brightly, my love. Now rest, high on the passion of the Priestess who has reclaimed her art.

For Your Consideration: As the Moon Grows...

Consider this: The waxing moonlight casts a milky glow on your soul's path, illuminating your next steps. Ask yourself these pertinent questions, and be sure to listen deeply to your inner Witch. She is concerned, above all else, with your soul's wandering path, for she wants your wildness to be fuel for purpose and fulfillment. Human beings across gender lines are told that discipline and control are the stuff of true success, but consider your wild liberation as the sharpest knife, positioned to slash through all that tethers and confines your greatest potential. Furthermore, consider the ebbs and flows of your many cycles as clues to your purpose in this sacred community of ours; if an area of your life is always waning when another is always waxing, what does this tell you of your path? If we are always unlearning limiting beliefs while gaining layers of knowledge that support our freedom, then what does your inner Witch have to say about uncovering the soul beneath the ego? Ask yourself these questions in a quiet space, and listen not for the loudest inner voice; listen to the soft whisper of the womb-heart as she answers.

1. What area of your life is waxing right now? Financial abundance? Sensuality and self-care? Sacred work? Love? Voice? Creativity? Spirituality?

2. What area of your life is in a period of fullness? You'll feel this fullness as pure power. This is an area of your life in which you feel you are a formidable force of nature, unstoppable even in the face of adversity.

3. What area of your life is waning, forcing you to let go of something? This letting-go part of the cycle demands acceptance and grace, even when the *thing* you are releasing weighed on your freedom.

4. Now, and this may be challenging, my Sister, what area of your life is in a dark moon phase right now? You are no longer letting go but rather sinking into a void of sorts. The dark moon period tends to be marked by fear that this *thing* that is gone may never

return, that the black of midnight will endure forever, but this, dear Witch, is not the case.

5. Finally, choose the area of your life that seems most pertinent to your soul's purpose right now, regardless of which cyclical phase that area may be in. Harvest your memories, seeing if you can trace a cycle of waxing, fullness, waning, and darkness. Have you lived through a full cycle yet? If so, how many months or years did the phases last? Can you predict any future phases, and, if so, what can you do to prepare for this transformation?

Women often have an undernourished need to take stock of the deep self, and, when they do, such assessments can be unwittingly bound to supposed-tos and can result in the automatic scrawling of angry to-do lists that overburden and severely demotivate. Your wild woman spirituality serves you well in these soul-centered evaluations, for the voice of judgment is quieted by the songs of the feminine divine. How can you be so wrong or off the mark if you are the essence of the cosmos? The moon does not berate herself as she wanes, digging her lunar claws into the past, weeping for how beautiful she was when she was full. The natural fallow times are just as honorable as your phases of abundance, my love, and your inner Witch and wild woman know this well. Be patient, and know that all is coming.

THE FULL MOON'S FRUITION
Your Lunar Summer

Ah, the bright full moon! You have felt this lunar phase more strongly than all the other moon seasons. The full moon powers the waters of this Earth, and the land-to-water ratio on our great planet nearly mirrors that inside your own body. Your woman's tidal rhythms beat the loudest when the moon is full, and it is at this time when your creative sensual power and the divine feminine energy of relationship is the strongest. The full moon is summer returning every month, even in the dead of the solar winter season, and harnessing the magick of this fullness is your feminine birthright.

The energy of the full moon can be fearsome, truth be told, and cognizance of this phase is integral to your life as a Woman Most Wild. The full moon will call you out of the broom closet with a siren song so eerily serene that you cannot help but answer. This lunar phase is one of completion and fruition, when the fragile *new* you have been so carefully nurturing begins to ripen toward birth. The full moon will not always act in ways you perceive as favorable; She is following Her own program, after all. These so-bright moons will put you back on your soul's path if you have lost your way, often dragging into the light what has been kept in the shadows.

Mystery and magick vibrate palpably in a night lit so blindingly by the full moon. Spellwork is at its most effective, and the call to wild sisterhood may be strong. You will feel a deeply seated internal need for balance during the full moon, as your woman's waters succumb to the moon's pull. I say, let the full moon take you. Any emotions that surface, any desires that seem irrational, any feminine impulse that bites at you from the inside: Do not fight these forces under the full moon. Allow the magick to surge through you. Bathe in moonlight, and sense the wholeness of your so-illumined heart.

Learning to harness full moon energy to infuse sacred work and meaningful relationships is an integral component of the wild woman's curriculum. The full moon does not exist to serve you, my love, no more than you exist to serve it. The relationship between the Witch and the moon, be it full or at any other cyclical point, is one of mutual reverence and energetic connection. The greatest lesson the full moon teaches us every month is this: Your sensuality and creativity are holy, and there is as much divinity in the erotic as there is in any prayer. The wild woman is tasked with a great unlearning, for she must untangle the knotted twine formed from millennia of profound distrust and strategic suppression of her sexual and generative power. She must unbind wrappings on her sex and spirit, if only to see what lies beneath the tethers others have placed on her.

Moonbathing with the Maiden: The Full Moon and Erotic Innocence

A woman seeking to embody sacred sensuality is challenged to undo not only her own sexual woundings but also those sourced from thousands of years of collective feminine subjugation. Your path toward sensual wholeness is different from mine, my Sister, and I am not so arrogant as to prescribe a specific regimen for you. Erotic innocence is not a goal but a practice, and a necessary one at that. We live in a pivotal age of transformation in which the mysteries of women's subtle and heavy bodies are being brought to light; and yet, these positive shifts are contextualized within a shadowy soup of media-supported body shaming.

Go into the night now, as a Witch most sensual. Seek out a darkened place underneath the shield of trees if you must, but look for places where the full moon casts its milk-gray glow on a space, however small. If you cannot be outdoors, go into your home's wild sanctuary and attune to the lunar energy around you. Sit in the moonlight now, Priestess. Let the light penetrate your deepest sacral wound, be it scarred over or still bleeding. Give permission to the lunar light to seep into the voids within your would-be sensual wholeness, and invite the moonlight to electrify the Maiden within. Be who you were born to be, as if you were raised within the Red Tent, a place of historic menstrual support, where all the mothers and grandmothers of this world encircle you and validate your feminine blood as holy. Place both palms flat on your womb-center and affirm thrice: *I am Maiden, and I am whole.* Whatever your woundings, my love, you are flawless in your soul, body, mind, and spirit. You are not broken. You are not incomplete. You are the wild perfection of all things on and beyond this great Earth of ours. Even if you do not have a physical womb, that fertile space of life, death, and creative power remains inside you, in all its energetic glory.

The womb-wounds of women are often the best-kept secrets. In circles of women where the space is safely held, stories of lost pregnancies, infertility, hysterectomies, and, most commonly, abuse in its myriad forms are often unleashed in an eruption of long-dammed pain. There comes a time, I believe, in every woman's life when a harvesting of these truths must come. If verbally sharing your story is too painful or would only cause a deeper wounding, write it down, shunning perfection and shame, then burn the pages. Seek out professional support and safe, healing spaces. The act of lifting these experiences out of their sacral depths raises their vibration, permits them to be less manifest as a binding agent to your soul, and brings them into the light. Women who share their sexual stories often begin by believing their story means little, and then in the sharing begin to know the weight of their past and the extent to which it has kept them immobile. A great release comes from the telling, as if a heavy, dreadful *something* was keeping a critical part of their soul static until their voice could be heard.

Know that you have been infallible in every decision you have made. You are blameless and perfect as you are, in this moment, and you always have been so. There can be no misstep when you are sacred and whole, and, my love, you are both of these, forever and always.

Verses of the Holy Feminine
A Full Moon Prayer of Gratitude and Surrender

For all I am about to receive on this blessed, holy night, I am truly thankful. Hear my open-hearted and open-legged prayer to the silver moon, Great Mystery, for this child of the universe is wide awake. I will not turn away from the fertile wild, for I have found my true worth. I have tasted the blissful sweetness of river water and rose petals, and I have cut myself on the thorns of raw, red, running beauty. My blood is my war paint, and I am going to battle for you.

Thank you for the scent of fresh snow, new blooms, hot rain, and leaf rot. Thank you for all tastes, for my tongue has licked the hearty roots of soul, the cool mint of spirit, and everything in between. Thank you for my strong bones and my belly fire. Thank you for my sensual divinity and holy sexuality. My cup runneth over with the raw emerald-green heart light of empathic connection and feminine generosity. I am giving it all to you, Mystery; take me, I am yours.

I am surrendering the wisdom of the cosmos, but I am affirming my sacred role in the Great Turning. I hold all the magick of this wounded world within my womb, and I have sunk my teeth deeply into the burning bone marrow of human transformation. I have swum against the tide for a time, and now I feel the current shifting, sucking the ancient sands of stagnant shame away from under my bare feet. I am finding new ground, and for this I am eternally thankful. From the bottom of my wild heart, all blessings be.

Weaning the Creatrix-Mother: The Guilt of Completion

Much of the fear pervading the full moon phase of the cycle stems from the guilt of completion. Recall, my love, a time in your life when you were creatrix, birthing something into being for which you cared dearly. As your creation neared fruition, you likely experienced a fair amount of trepidation. The end was finally in sight, and now you were poised to be released from your role as Creatrix-Mother. Depending on how closely you identified with this role, you may have needed to reorder your very identity.

The task of the full moon phase of the cycle is to be as fully and unapologetically present as possible. When an intense generative fire burns in a woman's belly, she does well to create solely for creation's sake. In *What We Ache For*, Oriah Mountain Dreamer tasks the artist with trusting the process as wholly as she or he can: "We must be faithful — full of faith that the process of creating will be enough to feed us and the world." The trust of the Creatrix-Mother comes from the understanding that, though the inevitable letting go is coming, the cyclical nature of all things is ever-turning.

The full moon begs us to balance the guilt of completion, the sense that maybe we have somehow misstepped or wronged our creation, with a cyclical view of time. Feminine time is circular but specifically spiral and certainly not linear. You may well be facing the letting-go phase of some majestic thing now, but the essence of what you so lovingly mothered will be reborn into another incarnation soon. So, my Witch, revel in this phase of fullness and fruition, for it is the height of your creative, life-giving power.

THE WANING MOON'S EVE OF ACCEPTANCE
Your Lunar Autumn

Every Witch is different, but I find the happiest wild women are those who relish the opportunity to let entire phases of their lives die out, like flowers withering under the first frost. The waning moon is a space maker, a field clearer, and a massive, high-powered declutterer; it calls you to accept the loss of what is already leaving you as preparation for the dark moon void.

Your lunar autumn is a time of release and boundary creation. You must honor the earlier aspects of the lunar cycle for how they served you, birthing what needed to be birthed and then dancing in celebration of completion, but this is not where the challenge lies. You must then death-doula yourself through the process of accepting loss. As the moon wanes, the natural world experiences a sense of imminent darkness, a darkness that we have been conditioned to fear.

Look to the waning moon, Wild One, as a great organizer. The energy of Mother Moon ebbing toward darkness is much like that of the destructive Goddesses, such as Kali in the Hindu tradition or the Cailleach in Celtic wisdom; She clears the fields to make space for what will come. Swallow the changes lit by the waning moon as necessary progressions toward your soul's destiny. Use this time to learn how to see in the dark, and open your third eye wide.

Women are taught to resist these phases of letting go and the empty void. In a culture that fervently emphasizes productivity over nonaction, we are socialized to dig our metaphoric fangs deeply into anything that is in the process of leaving us. We want it all, but we deserve space as much as we deserve the abundance of *having*. What if we are always letting go of something in order to make space for the new? What if, in the balance, we are perfectly supported by the great swell and the great purge at any given point in our lives?

Women need and deserve the fallow time. Go into the dark regularly and fearlessly, holding steadfast in the knowledge that you are not meant to be the ever-generative Creatrix-Mother at all times. Permit yourself to be reborn in the dark; relinquish roles, practices, and relationships that no longer serve. Embrace sweet solitude as a means of evaluation. We see ourselves far more clearly in the dark than we do in the light, Sister, and you know this to be true.

The Witch in the Dark: Psychic Shielding for Wild Women

The waning lunar phase is a pivotal time for psychic development and honing your subtle-energy sight. As close to midnight as possible, and in a room where you will not be disturbed, sit quietly in the shadowy silence, with your eyes wide open. Draw a slow spiral in both of your palms with a fingertip, and feel your palm chakras open wide. Now, psychic Witch, place your hands together in front of you, slowly moving them away from one another and then back toward each other until you feel just the smallest bit of resistance between your palms. Look at your hands with soft vision, a sacred gaze, a drishti. Do you see it? A foggy blue-white glow emanates from your hands now; you are seeing your body's very life-force. You are witnessing your own prana in action, your electricity, the very juice of your aura.

You have been told, dear Witch, from the time you were young, that such subtle energies are not real, and you have unlearned seeing them out of social necessity. Not wanting to be ostracized, you unconsciously denied that this sea of energy exists all around us. Here, in this soft, glowing soup, you can learn to see angels, guides, and spirits. Here you will break down the patterns of vision you have learned, dismantling years of conditioning. Here you will truly begin to see in the dark.

Close your eyes now, my Sister-Witch. Become aware of that same glowing energy field you witnessed around your hands. Know it now as vibrating all around you, extending away from you several feet in all directions. Envision this now: On the outermost edge of this aura of yours is a hard, quartz-crystal shell. This shield is permeable only in one direction; you can send energy out, if you wish, but nothing can enter your aura from the outside. Nest in the safety of your psychic shield now, great armored Priestess, and use this protective skill whenever you are feeling vulnerable to psychic or emotional attack. Strong boundaries are a Witch's best friend, and you will learn to use them well, my love.

Psychic shielding is a practice that will support you not only in your Craft but also in day-to-day living. Many women are awakening to the burden of the empath in our society. Empathy, on the one hand, is a much needed quality of the Wild Healer Archetype, with feelings being absorbed and assimilated by one human from another. Anodea Judith defines empathy in *The Global Heart Awakens* as the "building block of compassion....Here we drop all judgment and preoccupation with our own dramas." On the other hand, overly empathic individuals of all genders may feel regularly consumed by the emotional energies of others, much to their own psychological confusion and physiological depletion. When you hone your skills in boundary creation, you do yourself a formidable service in protecting your sacred self against both malicious and unwitting trespassers. A woman who nurtures herself so nurtures every woman in the world. So may it be for you, and so may it be for every one of us.

THE DARK MOON AND NESTING IN NOTHINGNESS

Closely associated with the aspects of the feminine that have been most feared, most condemned throughout time, the dark moon phase is marked by a lunar void. This phase, my brave Witch, is your lunar winter. Here you are a seed resting in the deep soil, waiting for the spark of life to ignite an inevitable stir in your heart. The dark of the moon is a time of seeming finality and death, and it is associated with your inner Wise Woman, an all-knowing Witch consciousness that lives in quiet solitude and perfect stillness.

At the dark of the moon, my love, it is best to work no manifestation magick unless you feel called loudly to work. Now is the time for clear seeing, divine reception, and surrender. Rituals and self-designed ceremonies marking transitions, validating cyclical conclusions, or supporting feminine intuition are ideal for this psychically fertile phase of the moon. Sink into the void with all that you are, and relish this time of thick, psychic energy and nourishing rest. Take time to be alone during those nights when the moon seems to be abandoning the world. Consider what you may be grieving for. Ask yourself: What has been released from your life during this past lunar month? Have you truly accepted this change?

The Witch of the Dark Moon embodies a subtle reverence for nothingness and stillness. She looks neither ahead nor behind her. She resists the urge to plan and perfect, and, in that empty space, she becomes a receptor for tiny pinpoints of light, divine nudges, and infinitesimal hints that she collects in a psychic knapsack. She does not try to order this information or make too much sense of it; she simply gathers, giving herself permission to feel her way through the dark by the power of her keenest senses.

The Nine of Swords: A Dark Moon Ritual

The levels of grief are both complex and personal. As women we are often taught to suppress our emotions for fear of being perceived as weak, and depression, we learn, is unforgivable. Women's deep dive into periods of sadness, lethargy, and complete surrender is often a necessary time of respite. Something is not working in your life, be it physically, emotionally, or spiritually, and depression groundswells from your feminine roots in an effort to pull you down into urgently needed contemplation. Here, in your dark night of the Witch's soul, you give yourself permission to feel it all. You will weep and let the tears have their way with you.

The nine of swords in a Tarot deck marks a woman in pain; very often she is affected by quintessential wounds of the feminine. Ponder this, love: If you were asked to be the creatrix of a ritual, a self-designed ceremony of letting go, what would you dedicate this ritual to? In the darkness of this moon, design a sacred ceremony of release and transition that will give you time and space both to acknowledge loss and to welcome transformation.

Light a white candle and burn sage and sweetgrass. Whisper now the intention for this ritual: *Tonight, I am marking the end/death/ release/conclusion of _____. I offer gratitude for how I was served by this powerful force when it was in my life, but now I am letting it go. I accept this change and give myself permission to feel the emotions deep in my womb.* Let these feelings bloom and bubble from within you in whatever way seems fitting, for as long as you have. You will know when the ritual is complete, my love, for you will feel a tingle of rebirth; you will find a small bit of space into which you can nestle, one that was not there at the ceremony's inception.

Snuff out the candle and sink into an unburdened sleep, waking just as the new moon dawns. Do not try too hard to label your emotions, positive or negative, for our language very often has no words for the complexity of our feelings. In this dark moon space, simply acknowledge that a change has occurred, feel supported by the gift of ground beneath you, and breathe. Know that just enough psychic clutter has been cleared to offer you a window through which you can look, wielding the fierce foresight of a mother hawk.

The wild woman is adept at quieting the urge to label and quantify the changes occurring both within and outside her being. You may not feel immediate shifts following rituals and magick work, but you must know in your bones that you have done all you can. Though we have nothing to call this particular transformation, this small bit of space making you have done, the insufficiency of our language does not diminish the weight of your work. I find that when I have no names for how I feel after a ritual, the greatest shifts are just on the horizon.

Contemplating True Vision: Wild Divination

The restlessness of the dark moon phase can be remedied by practices of divination. Go into nature, wild woman that you are, and gather small objects that speak to your soul; these might be seeds, twigs, shells, bones, rocks, eggshells, or anything else that you can hold in your hand. Place each of these in a bag, box, or other container that seems magickal. Find a place outdoors where you will not be disturbed, or go into your home's wild sanctuary, ideally at night when the moon is dark.

Now, sacred Sister, ask your inner Witch to speak to you of a crucial area in your life right now. Is it your work? Your relationship? She will answer you, my love. Give her a moment. Focusing on that life area with a laser-point intention, cast your wild objects in front of you. Perhaps it feels right to pour them onto the ground in a spiral motion, or to throw them into the distance. Whatever seems right, do it. Now look. What are these unlabeled runes telling you? What is your initial response to how these things are arranged? What object stands out the most? How are the objects connected, if at all? What does this wild spread tell you of your life?

Use wild divination as a bucket to draw from the deep well of your intuition. Consider that you already know everything you are meant to know at any given moment, but there are so many demands on our attention that we do not often look inward. Our animal brains are designed to protect us first from physical threats; the subtle becomes suppressed by the heavy and the physical. Focusing on whatever vehicle you use for the purposes of divining does not gift you with anything you do not already know; it simply clarifies, pulling from the shadows and making visible what otherwise would be easily ignored. A wild woman can divine as easily from a sink full of dirty dishes or a bit of sidewalk gum as she can from a gold-embossed oracle deck. See magick in the mundane, and know yourself as Witch.

THE SACRED MARRIAGE OF THE FEMININE MOON AND THE MASCULINE SUN

You may liken lunar wisdom to that of a wise grandmother. The moon is maternal and offers you hearty but subtle nourishment. By contrast, solar energies are paternal, heated, and active. The marriage of the moon and sun sustains the whole of your being as a daughter of the cosmos. Know that I use these parental terms less to refer to gender and more to refer to the feminine and masculine aspects within our human psyches. You, child of the moon and stars, must honor your alignment with both the fertile darkness of the night and the vibrant light of day. You are everything. Everything is you. Awaken your lunar memory, and embrace your birthright. Claim the sign of the multiphased moon as a symbol of wild womanhood, and plant that symbol deep in your Maiden's sensual womb, your Mother's creative belly, and your Crone's intuitive third eye. My Sister, they will not see you coming, for you are truly and madly a Woman Most Wild.

Chapter 2

The Righteous Sun
and Your Priestess's Fire

*I*f the moon is your temple dancer's silver-charmed sheer skirts, the sun is your bejeweled Priestess's crown. The sun has no patience for mystery or shadow; it is a brilliant beacon of the unrelenting spiral of time. Your solar-season cycles are far lengthier than your lunar cycles, but their impact is no less profound on your psyche. While the moon calls you to surrender to your soul's purpose on Earth, the sun begs you to remember your role in the cosmic dance. You, stellar Witch, are reveling in perfect rhythm with the astral plane. You are star-stuff. Feel how these solar cycles live in your body, not subtly as the moon cycles do but actively and often without apology. To ignore the sun's cycles is to be partially asleep, so open your mouth skyward and feel the heat on your tongue. Solar magick is spirit magick, and your inner Sun-Priestess remembers why.

In this chapter I offer you dream visions of seasonal transitions, rituals and meditations for living in alignment with these solar cycles, and glimpses into how the broad spiral of solar time shapes wild woman spirituality. While you may resonate more with the description of the season during which you are reading this, consider all seasons within the ever-turning wheel of the solar year. An understanding of how winter's whispered voice begs you to rest will add much to your lived experience of summer's sultry song. The seasons do not exist in a vacuum; they are points on a cyclical and enduring journey that is at once futuristic and ancient.

Before reading this chapter, take a moment to recall how your body and mind greeted the seasonal transitions during your girlhood. Close your eyes and remember the natural omens of solar change: the morning birds in spring, the late-evening sunset in summer, the dim rays shining through a nearly bare tree in autumn, and the chill of sunlessness on your cheeks in winter. These brief moments of pure presence alerted you to your place in the ecological turning of the wild wheel. You knew in your bones that you were a single pulse beat within the many-hearted Mother, and there was much soft-breasted comfort in that knowing.

THE WINTER WITCH
Claiming Your Rest

A woman struggles deeply when the ways of the social world contrast sharply with the rhythms of nature. The Witch in winter faces a powerful social challenge; while all the world is bustling to commemorate various holidays with gift giving and candlelit perfection, the natural world is bidding you to come to bed. The winter solstice marks the longest night of the year, with the dawn after this long night deserving of immense gratitude. The rhythms of winter are slow and dark. You are a Goddess on the nest at this time, and it is normal to reject the intensity with which our consumer culture urges you to act. Move slowly and with purpose, winter Witch. Do not create that vision board just yet. Claim your rest, and know that all is waiting for you by the light of day.

The Return of the Light: A Yuletide Ritual for a Witch Most Tired

Carve out a bit of space and time for yourself on the winter solstice, my love. Draw the curtains, and go into your cave. Light no candles, and cast no spells. Let yourself be in a space of absolute darkness. In your left hand, hold a box of matches and feel the vibrant possibility of fire. Know the power of this sacred blaze's potential, though it has not yet been realized. Relish the honor of being a fire keeper. Center your consciousness at your crown, and recall ancient memories of your ancestors, who stood within stone circles or other ritualistic spaces, awaiting the sunrise on this very day. Let a quiver of fear run through your bones, just as it ran through theirs: Will the sun truly return? Will life carry on? Is there an end to this enduring night? Honor these queries as primitive fuel for your flame now, and strike a single match.

The blaze illuminates your beauteous face and fills in the crevices around your tired eyes. The warmth of this flame, from the core of the Earth to the core of your belly to the core of the blessed sun, is the same as that which melted the trepidations of those in your bloodline. This flame is your inner dawn. Open to it, and drink in the spicy magick of a single flame lit within the blackness of winter. Let it nourish you, for you do not need much right now. This single flame is enough. Feel its warmth on your fingers, and then snuff it out just as the winter sun rises pink in a cold gray sky.

Now to bed, my love. Claim those last few moments of sleep, for the day will wait for you. You are a Witch most tired, and all your ancestral grandmothers want to tuck you into a warm bed. Lay your head heavy on a lavender-scented pillow, and feel your room surrounded by the spirits of sleep. Let them lull you into a snowy dreamland where all the presents have been wrapped, the meals have been cooked, the parties have been attended, and there is nothing more for you to do. You are neither consumer nor producer in sleep; you are simply a tired woman, claiming her right to rest. Hear the voices of the hooded ones as they sing you whispered lullabies and remind you, once again, of who you truly are.

Find an ancient solace in the smallest bit of firelight. Women understand the promise of the light's return, for we have all been lonely lovers staring at a mass of black water and night sky, waiting for the return of a great something that has left us in our depths. The winter solstice is a time to wait without expectation, to rest without a plan to move, and to trust the infinite Mystery. A candle lit within a dark room is a harbinger of the yet-to-come, and small rituals like these do much to warm the heart weary of the wait.

Gift for the Miracle Mother: A Guided Meditation

Let this pathwork gift you with a renewed sense of purpose as winter waxes. In your dreams, you come to a frozen land. Your breath fogs in the cold, but your body is oddly warm in this frost-laden snowscape. The field before you is covered with a layer of virgin snow, whole unto itself, and the full moon glitters on the bare branches of the mighty oaks to your right. To your left is an uninviting cave entrance, the stone covered in moss-filled carvings of ancient symbols. To your Witch's mind, they appear to be symbols of protection.

Dull light flickers from inside this subterranean space, and despite the entryway's jagged, toothy images, you feel called to go inside. Move stealthily now, winter Witch, and listen intently to your belly brain. You do not know what waits for you inside, my love, so be guarded. Once inside, you are aware that the cave is quite large, though you duck the dripping, crystalline stalactite formations. The cave smells thickly of cold mud and contains an ancient, mythic memory. Firelight flickers from a still-distant place, and you begin to hear voices of the Old Ones. They echo stories of the miracle children, beings of light come to herald humanity's evolution; these famed ones came too early, the voices tell you, and their sacred messages were nurtured inside their mother's wombs long before those souls spoke to any crowd.

The light grows brighter as the voices grow quieter, and you find the source of the flame. She lies on a birthing bed most holy, surrounded by those who worship Her not because of what she holds in Her womb but because of Her own magnificence. This is the Mother of Miracles, dear one, and She begs you to trust your part in global transformation. Her labor has endured for millennia, and She is birthing the whole of the cosmos into being. Fall to your knees, Witch, and gaze upon this sacred moment. Today is our birthday, yours and mine, and this is our Mother. Look to Her birthing bed, my love, and know that all the blood that has been spilled, in every war and every horrific ego-born massacre, has been part of Her labor.

Gaze at the light dawning between the Miracle Mother's legs, and let your eyes weep for the beauty that is coming. We wild women stand at the precipice of a new feminine age. We are witnesses to awakened humanity's baby naming. This is it. Feel the warmth of enlightenment on your bare skin, and offer a gift to the Miracle Mother. What do you have for Her? What is your soul-designed purpose in this life? Cup your divine spark in your hands, and crouch at the Mother's side. You are overcome by the gratitude emanating from Her eyes as you offer Her your soul's gift. She has been waiting for you. Be Her midwife now as She enters the final stages of birthing our light into the dark. Do not feel you are unworthy, Gift Giver, for you are the one She needs at Her side now. You are the one for whom She has been waiting.

At this pivotal moment, women everywhere are waking to their designated task as wild healers of our wounded world. Know yourself as the Mother of Miracles, and trust your passions and desires as sacred clues to your purpose in this life. Make no mistake, Sister, you have been born for a reason, and the greatest change agent on our planet is a woman speaking her truth, telling her story, and fulfilling her divine mandate freely and without apology. Bill Plotkin writes in *Soulcraft* that "if, over time, you patiently hold your soul story within the context of your world story, at some point they will merge like a puzzle piece fitting into a greater mystery." Women who carefully shape the landscape of their individual lives now, as our human community shivers in its own dark, cold winter gripped by ego and war, do much to nourish the fertile green Motherland that will flourish in warmer days. By the light of day, all is coming.

The Woman in Late Winter

The woman in late winter is building a bridge between her third eye's intuition and the sensuality of her sacral chakra; such construction requires multiple resources, not the least of which are her time and energy. The doldrums of late winter can weigh heavy on a woman's shoulders when she is not permitted the space needed to engage her intuition and sensuality. She is overburdened by careful planning and strategic goal setting for the coming warmer season, when the very foundations for her spring have yet to be poured. Open spaces in late winter for pan-sensory being; feel the heavy wet flakes of the last snows on your skin, taste the melting icicles, breathe in the scent of iron-thick mud, hear the sounds of the night creatures, and see with three eyes. If you have even a few moments when nothing needs to be forced, use that time simply to *be*.

THE SPRING WITCH
Engaging the Sensual

Your Witch consciousness, centered in your sacrum, experiences a sensual ignition when the days grow warmer. Even if you live in an urban location surrounded by built structures and concrete, Gaia calls to you from below. Spring Witch, it is in your blood to nourish something green and make it grow at this time. It will serve you well to spend as much time outdoors as you can, for your skin is thirsty for the warmth of sunbeams and the mist of a soft rain. Spring boasts a waxing sensuality that the other seasons do not share; it is the time of the awakened womb, creative spark, and resonating life-force. Your inner Witch is a medium for pure prana as the wheel turns away from winter toward spring, and you may feel so alive that to continue with winter's tasks and schedules seems a dark and heavy burden. Engage the part of your magickal psyche that yearns for the new at this time, for your deep-seated Gypsy's soul must be fed during these warmer days.

Crystal Planting: A Healing Spell for Earth Day

Wild woman, we have been born into this world with the same sacred wound; every time our Earth is carved, shredded, and denigrated, we feel Her pain within our bodies. Our feminine psychic lands are riddled with rage and grief over the harm done daily to our Mother, and we suffer largely in silence. Each time a tree is dug up from the root or a river is polluted with harsh chemical distortions, our own cells cry out for both mercy and justice. One of the great falsehoods accepted by the human community is that one person cannot possibly make a difference in global healing, but this, my love, is a lie born of fear.

You are the very embodiment of the feminine divine; this power lives inside you, positioned for you to wield it as you will. Our great responsibility as children of Gaia, at this pivotal moment in human history, is to use our magick for global transformation. Do not play small, you fierce Woman, for you are fighting for your home. Go to a wild place now, bring a quartz crystal you have soaked in moonlight, and find a Mother Tree. If you are unable to go into nature, hold a crystal in your hand and proceed as if this were a meditation.

You know the Mother Tree when you see it, for it stretches over you like an aged faery grandmother. Hold the crystal in your left hand and press your ear against the bark. Do you hear it? She speaks to you in the language of Gaia, and She tells you of Her hopes and fears. The Mother Tree's energy runs through like a primitive current, garnet-red, straight from Her roots to yours. She knows you are a wild wandering woman, and She recognizes your true soul. Your crystal begins to vibrate with the resonance of Her, and you plant the offering at the Mother Tree's base, watering it with your grateful tears.

Lie upon the ground now, dear one. Get mud in your hair and hike up your skirt. This is the true Mother's Day, and you can feel the sparks of sprouting seeds below you mirroring the swelling pinpoints of light in your womb, belly, and heart. Honor yourself now, my Sister-Witch, for you have found your soul's authentic home. Return to the Mother Tree whenever you feel trapped by the doldrums of daily life. Come back to lie upon the Earth whenever you need to feel held, and drink in the medicine of tree magick whenever you feel wounded. Know that She has endured through countless storms, and that She feels the same pain you do.

From the roots of the body to the roots of the Mother Tree, blessed be. Trees are the stuff of the hearty feminine, and so are we.

Liberating the Spring Snake: A Meditation for Removing the Creative Block

The denigration of the wild Earth is similarly damaging to women's creativity. Much like our natural world, generative creative power does not wish to be fenced in, welled up, or manicured. Your creative fire is raw and serpentine. Woman, do not fear the snake, for it does not fear you. As you read this, a serpent lies coiled at the base of your spine awaiting your call. Your pelvic bowl is her home and, while there are times when she must sleep, now is not that time. Your creative fire has awakened her, and she longs to slither up your backbone to your emerald-green heart center. She longs to be liberated; now call her to action.

The snake is your feminine creative power and, try as you might, you cannot contain her on these warmer days. Envision your greatest blockage to creating. Where does it exist in your body? What color is it? What temperature? Now send your magick snake there. Let it lick away at the blockage, weakening it with every flick of her flaming tongue. She writhes around the blockage without effort, and soon your greatest creative obstacle has been removed, eaten away by the power of the Holy Wild. She moves now to your heart center and divides in two, ringing around your arm bones and crawling into your Witch's hands. Your fingers are abuzz now with unbridled energy. You are an emblazoned creatrix, and now you must channel that jewel-orange power. Wild Witch, paint, write, cook, dance, or doodle. Make mud pies. Shape some clay. String some beads. Your snake is awake! Now keep her free for as long as you can.

We are taught to distrust the snake as a harbinger of evil. So, too, we are urged to suppress our sensuality. In *Goddesses in Everywoman*, Jean Shinoda Bolen writes that "every heroine must reclaim the power of the snake." The power of the snake is the power of the feminine life-force residing within the sacred sacrum. A woman who begins to awaken this serpentine force, particularly if it has lain dormant for many years, will start to push beyond her own safe boundaries as an artist. She will risk much, allowing herself to be seen as an unbridled, and thereby untamable, force in her own world. She will buck against structures of oppression, and she will refuse to let her sensuality be contained in a lidded basket any longer. Once the snake is awake, dear Sister, both your creativity and sensuality have been similarly licked alive.

The Woman in Late Spring

The woman in late spring is a woman whose passion has caught fire. Know this passion as the sacrum-spawned energies that fuel your sacred work, your many tasks, and a true, active peak in the soulful being-doing-being cycle. The same pressures on the woman's body and mind that pushed her in many directions during the winter season may well persist into spring, but her psyche is often better equipped to prioritize and negotiate these to-dos as the wheel turns toward the hot southern gate of summer. There is more light in our lives, and we may well need less rest. As a woman moves into summer, she is served best by engaging in movement alchemy, purposefully wielding her body as an essential and integral part of the sacred self. Channel the building solar energies through your body; shake and jiggle in ways you never have before, unwind the knots in your joints, and make a hell of a lot of noise while you do it. The woman in late spring prepares to embody everything, and pulling the consciousness down into the lower chakras creates support for physical pattern breaking; it is a time of making your inner temple ready for the sun to move in, a time when the soft body serves you just as much as, if not far better than, the hard-thinking mind.

THE SUMMER WITCH
Heating the Cauldron

As the wheel turns from spring to summer, the Witch becomes a sheer force of fem-fire. She is a solar storm, and she must remember to nurture herself with cooling magick amid the heat of hedonistic play in the natural world. You can feel summer's wildfire in your boiling blood, my Sister-Witch, and you have the power to burn down the parts of your world now that no longer serve you. Prepare to clear the fields, my love. Harvest all that will feed you, and then plan to dig up what does not belong. Here, under the summer sun, your body is fully alive and poised for action. Drink in this spice with all that you are. Give yourself permission to be a wise Maiden, sexually empowered and spiritually attuned to all that is.

The woman during the summer months yearns to paint her world with the cool greens of the forest and the hot bright reds of a flower garden. She will no longer stand for the mundane and the dull, and she seeks to simplify her home and her life. There is a purifying quality to summer's heat that she recognizes immediately as a tool for the great purge, a tool that is hers to use as she will. The woman in summer is a creature born of the elements, and she seeks brilliance and fruition in all parts of her world; anything that does not meet these high standards she immediately recognizes as refuse, and she sets upon the path of clarity and release.

Faery Gazing: Night Vision in the Moon Garden

The Fae are nature spirits, and they are not to be discounted simply as tiny-winged, wish-granting beings of pure light. Just as humans do, the Fae embody both light and shadow, and they do not wish to be used as a magickal tool. If your Witch's psyche does not accept these Fae as real, energetic manifestations, consider these creatures a metaphor for humanity's culturally suppressed kinship with nature. The Fae, and you know this in your Witch's heart, are to be heralded as ancient entities who are very much of this Earth. They are as diverse as human beings, if not more so. They are beholden to no woman or man; and yet the Witch has a symbiotic relationship with these Old Ones. Do not fear them, but do respect them, my Sister-Witch, as you go into your garden, your in-home sanctuary, or an untouched, natural space.

The Fae are more heavily concentrated in spaces that human hands have left unbuilt and unmarked. Parks, wetlands, and protected mountainous terrains are the realms of the Fae, but any natural green space is likely to host a few of Gaia's direct descendants. The Fae are no strangers to urban locales, however; if you live in a highly populated location, seek out even small green spaces, searching for their energy. You will feel it, Sister, when you have found the right spot. *Yes. Yes, this is the place* will echo at your womb-center. Surrounded by the Fae, you are; look around with night vision. Do you see them? Let your gaze go soft and blurry, and begin to see the swirling subtle energies that elude you during the day. Turn your soulful eyes toward flowers and trees. Do you see the circles of soft light there? Does a spark of brilliance catch your attention and then vanish?

They are showing themselves to you, summer Witch! Let them know you see them with whatever affirmation comes to mind. Keep looking, and they will keep coming. Stay in this place for as long as you have. Your connection to the Fae has been forged! Now they will show themselves to you more often, even by the light of day. Drink in the sweet swelter of the summer night, and honor the beauty of the unseen.

A wild woman embodies an intuitive understanding of the ethereal world. She does not discount the possibility of the unseen, and she gives regular nods to the mystical. Even if you are not certain that you believe in the Fae, entertain the *maybe* in all things. Always keep some psychic room for the unknown, and remember that the structures of human society, particularly our religious institutions, which depended on a singular faith in a male deity or the infallibility of a sacred text in order to survive, have had much to gain from the closed-minded discounting of the subtle ethereal. You see what you believe in, my love. By extension, you see far more when you claim little certainty.

For Your Consideration: As the Cauldron Bubbles

The wild woman in summer cuts through futility like a hot knife through butter. You are beginning to know yourself now as my wild Sister and, as the heat of our great sun shines His fierce light on all aspects of your life, you are discovering parts of that life that no longer fit. Look to your life now and compare the things you invest your energy in with the things you truly love and desire. My barefoot Priestess, there should be no comparison, for they should be one and the same! Command your throne now at the campfire's edge, and consider these questions as your cauldron bubbles. Let the sweat form rivulets of change on your forehead, pulling out of your psychic shadows the hidden obstacles to your freedom. The sun sees all, my love, and now you do, too.

1. If your life were an epic myth titled *The Woman Most Wild*, what would the chapter titles be? Include chapters from your birth all the way up until your death ritual.

2. Within each of those lived chapters, list moments of *bhava*, moments when you were engaged in the feeling mind, when your body, mind, and spirit were fully present, fully connected, and fully engaged. These are the moments when you were most *you*. How many of these moments occurred in the natural world? How many occurred while you were in the midst of creating something? Are any natural elements (earth, water, fire, air, or ether) prominent?

3. What chapters in your life, if any, contain few or none of these moments? How many of these moments are in the current chapter of your life?

4. Now, my love, write the next chapter of your life in full. Forget grammar and spelling, and just freewrite this next phase of your life the way you want it to be. Your soul already holds a purpose, but you, Creatrix-Witch, are in charge of how that purpose will be delivered.

Begin this next chapter with these words: *She was a Woman Most Wild and, as summer came to an end, she knew in her bones that autumn promised change.* Write with all the fury of a spell well conjured, for the healing of the global community depends on you.

We women must shape our her-stories. Personal mythwork is an invaluable tool not only for uncovering your purpose but also for tracking cycles and providing contexts for moments of immense bliss and deep woundings. Writing your own story is immensely healing and the stuff of true soul work, for you begin to frame yourself as the heroine in the greatest love story ever told. Your story is my story, and it is a story of a woman coming home to herself again and again, weathering countless storms, having her ego softened by intense blows, and then healing from them in order to be reborn a more authentic version of herself.

The Woman in Late Summer

The last weeks of summer embody a perplexing quality, and there is a reason for this; as the wheel begins to turn toward autumn, the curtain between the heavy world of humans and the subtler, higher frequency world of spirits begins to lift. Women are particularly attuned to this veil-thinning, and there is a mournful essence to it. The intensity of summer begins to give way now to an immense psychic space, as if a lightning-born wildfire has come through and cleared a forest for new growth. The grief of late summer stems from a desire to fill any open space coupled with the current inability to do so. There is nothing to fill this void with right now. You must be truly and authentically *in* it with your whole soul.

THE AUTUMN WITCH
Digging through Ashes

A sexy sort of sadness comes with the falling leaves, autumn Witch. Not everyone can openly feel the relentlessness of the changing wind, but you can. Lift your hood but do not turn your back to the first fall chill, for this season of nature's sleep holds it *all* for you. As the great veil thins and the days grow shorter and shorter, your spirit guides will sing in unison with your long-gone ancestors, hoping you will hear them. You, Witch of the harvest moon, must now dig through the ashes of summer's fire. Give yourself over to this season, and let the autumn winds do with you as they will. The high-fire energy potent with the fertility of spring and summer is now waning, leaving much space for soul listening. You will feel bursts of intuition in these months; do not dismiss them, for your Witch consciousness is guiding you toward the next step in your soulful evolution.

Meeting the Soul-Mother: Pathworking as the Veil Thins

There is magick in your matrilineal bloodline. Breathe now as if the spaces between the inhales and exhales lasted an eternity, as if you could live an entire life in that time at the top of the in-breath and at the bottom of the out-breath. It is within those between spaces of breath-fulness and breathlessness where you will find Her. As you sink into your breath's ancient rhythm, let the beat of your heart-drum herald Her coming.

Imagine yourself standing now within a stone circle, each mega-lith carved with the language of your ancestors. You can almost read it, for your blood remembers. Here, as the gray autumn sky swirls in soft spirals, the hairs on your arms stand upright. Your Witch's body is elec-trified by the energy of the divine feminine, and you sense Her presence long before your eyes find Her.

Who is this Mother of your Soul, autumn Witch? What age does She seem to be? How is She clothed, if at all? Does she appear human or otherworldly? Now, my love, ask Her these questions, knowing She will only offer answers She believes you are ready for: *Mother, how long have you been with me? What is your name? What is my soul's purpose? What is my purpose in this life? What do I need to know most right now?* Ask your Soul-Mother anything else you wish to know right now. Perhaps

She has a gift for you; perhaps Her gift to you is Her guidance. Finally, ask your Soul-Mother how you will know when She is around you. Is there a sign She can give you when She is near? Perhaps bells will chime from an unknown source, a bird will call to you, or you will see an unexplained pinprick of light.

Knowing that this Soul-Mother is always with you, bid Her farewell in whatever way seems appropriate. It may be a fierce, maternal embrace or a mere nod. Remember, not all Mother-Daughter relationships are marked by warmth. She leaves you now with greater knowledge of your soul's purpose in this world. She leaves you in sacred space, and you return your attention to your heartbeat and the breath spaces. Having met your Soul-Mother, return to your life more whole and well-nourished, affirming this point in the cycle of transformation as soul designed and predestined.

Learn to trust your collective of spirit guides, even if you find it difficult to communicate with them initially. Know that they are here for you, and that wild woman spirituality is undergirded by a fierce trust in the Mystery. You may not see your team of angels, but know that they are there.

The Dumb Supper: A Ritual of Remembrance for Those in Spirit

Under these darkening skies, you are acutely attuned to all the losses you have experienced. We have lost those who have shaped our feminine power through actions marked by both good and ill intent. We have lost mentors, friends, children, blood family, and found family. As the Great Wheel begins to turn toward winter and the nights grow long and ghostly, the Witch begins to experience these losses more as transitions. Honor those in the realm of Spirit, my love, for they are waiting to sit with you once again.

Set the grandest table you can; the spirits deserve it, after all. Light tall taper candles that drip wax over dried flowers and bones. Set places for the living and the dead. Dish out their favorite foods, speak words of remembrance, and play their favorite songs without speaking. The

Dumb Supper is a ritual of solemn remembrance. Let the dinner drift naturally into silence. Can you hear them? They are whispering words of sheer gratitude. Do not be afraid, Spirit-Walker, for they have always been there; now you are aware of their presence. They know you have wept for them, and they, too, have grieved for the loss of their human lives. Your loved ones are not lost. They wait for you beyond the veil, and you will see them again.

On this night, take their full plates outside and leave them overnight as an offering to those in Spirit. Listen for them as you go to sleep, and dream of candlelit vigils for ancestors you have never met in this life. Sink deep into the solace of the dark moon, for death is but a place on the never-ending spiral of life.

Autumn is the season of the death ritual. For all humans, giving an affirming nod to death creates a more meaningful relationship with life. Western culture encourages us to turn a blind eye to the inevitable end that waits for these bodies of ours, and this short-sightedness robs us of living more authentically in the present. A subtle, intermittent knowing that they could die at any moment shapes the lives of wild women, and rituals of remembrance serve as invaluable opportunities for living more fully — and with a good deal of hedonistic enjoyment.

The Woman in Late Autumn

A quiet thirst for three waters dries the throat of a woman in late autumn; she needs to drink from the cool river of feminine independence more at this time of year, spending far more time alone than she did in the summer months. So, too, she needs to drink from the wellspring of mourning and loss, acknowledging, with ritual and remembrance, those people and things that have gone from her life. Finally, in necessary preparation for the resting-in-darkness phase of winter, a woman in late autumn must attend to her intuition by engaging the subtle senses. Look for what you were told was not there, and listen for the voices you were told you did not hear.

Verses of the Holy Feminine
The Song of the Ever-Dying, Ever-Living God-Star

I am homesick for a state of undying grace. I yearn for the eternal warmth of the sacred masculine's strong arms, and I weep with the heartfelt knowledge that my ever-dying God-Star leaves me in the soft-breasted embrace of the moonlight each night but returns to my bed before I open my eyes. I fall to my knees and gasp when I see the two of you, my luscious lunar soul and vibrant solar spirit, in the same sky in late afternoon, and I yearn for the two of you to stay just that way, in perfect balance, in perfect trust, in perfect union.

I am homesick, as the day wanes, for the feeling state of your pure acceptance. On this day, my so-bright love, I do not want you to go! Come to bed with me in the dark, just this once, and I will have the ascended masters write you a pardon. Let me feel your fire on my face while I sleep, and She, our blessed moon, will watch from above while we break all the rules. Let's cause a scandal, my God-Star, my sun, for we are not really living if they are not whispering about us in quiet corners.

Cast your bright light on whatever shame I have left, you magnificent emblazoned beast, for with you I have nothing to hide. Let's burn our guilt at the stake and scatter its ashes over the sacred mountains of this world on a sunlit night. I fear nothing in your holy beams, for you are the hottest desire I have ever had. Let me lick your corona, and I will show you where I keep my secrets buried. Pink my skin with your rays in my sleep, and I will wake a new woman.

Now that I have found you, part of me will ever burn. Blessed be the midnight sunbeams, and blessed be the wild sun.

YOUR WILD WOMAN'S DIVINITY

The magick of the solar year lies in its rhythmic, vibrant, in-your-eyes nature; you may have to squint at its brilliance until you get used to the shine. While we may too easily neglect the lunar phases because of their frequency, it is difficult to ignore the seasonal passage of time. You, Witch of the Sun and Moon, can feel both these great celestial bodies in your cells; with this knowledge comes an important understanding. You are the embodiment of the Triple Goddess. Living in rhythm with the sun and moon is a Tantric way of being in this world, and this marriage of action and reception, desire and surrender, magick and mystery will amplify your body, mind, and spirit. You, astral Priestess, are ready to harvest your Goddess nature and open to a great truth buried deep within your being: You are every woman who has ever lived, every woman who is still breathing, and every woman who is yet to be born. You, Divine Mother, are truly a Woman Most Wild.

Chapter 3

The Wild Feminine
and Your Blood Rhythms

*H*onoring the Goddess may call to mind romantic images of bowing, hooded masses chanting to statues made of mossy stone; such
memories are neither false nor impertinent, but I ask you first to consider your own Goddess nature. You, my love, are the very embodiment
of the feminine divine, or what I will call the Shakti or She-Magick. In
this chapter we will explore how the ebbs and flows of your Goddess
nature reflect the same dance enacted by the sun and moon and undergird your emotions, identity, and all other ways of seeing your world.
As you read, you may feel a sharp inclination to dig your claws deeply
into an outmoded notion of the self. It requires a considerable loss of
control to know that parts of you are ultimately wild, but it demands
far more of you to know yourself as holy and divine. You are at once
a Maiden, a Mother, and a Wise Elder, and every month you are effectively birthing the whole world into being. In your womb, you hold the

power over both life and death and, for this very reason, the feminine has been deeply feared.

A woman coming to know her Goddess nature may well face a full-fledged identity crisis as she begins to dismantle deeply seated notions of deity as something that is external and superior to her being. She may begin to question indoctrinated belief systems and, to her credit, feel a good bit of anger at having been denied knowledge of her own divinity for much of her life. In *Sophia: Goddess of Wisdom, Bride of God*, Caitlín Matthews writes that "the West is exiled of the Goddess — her features are unknown to us, guessed at, hoped for, rejected as aberration, feared as monstrous or deformed." As young girls, we have an inborn memory of Goddess as Mother that slowly begins to crumble under the social needs of patriarchal religions. Religions respond to the requirements of the social structures that perpetuate and sustain them, with the major world religions rife with the desire to keep women powerless in order to maintain reverence to a male deity.

Women have been told they must live in spiritual poverty. Though the feminine is undoubtedly suppressed and denigrated in the dual realms of body and psyche within our masculine-oriented world, it is misogyny in the name of spirituality that does the worst damage. The loss of the spiritual self creates an unquenchable thirst for universal connection that manifests in addiction and other methods of escape. By extension, the suppression of the divine feminine is a deeply seated social mechanism for keeping women from being holistically nourished and fully present in their bodies, psyches, and spirits. You must consider the possibility that you are, in effect, the wild Goddess you have been waiting for since you were a young girl who prayed to the moon in secret.

As you begin to read this chapter, consider the divine source as a diamond-light, high-frequency energy that manifests in deity archetypes of all genders and in all forms. Consider it further as existing in your very cells, and recall your veneration for both nature and your own being when you were very young. As a girl, the body was magick just as a storm was magick. You knew yourself as a She-God then, though you did not articulate it that way, for you did not have to justify or explain such a profound and certain inner knowing. Recall a time when you felt positively limitless, when you felt infallible and invincible in your enduring spiritual nature. Harvest this memory now, and keep it close.

Dark Moon Maiden

The Maiden of the Dark Moon is the High Priestess of the Underworld. She exists in a void between death and birth, and She is marked by Mystery. Your Maiden phase harvests the She-Magick of psychic power, intuition, sensuality, and solitude; it exists at the dark of the moon and during the early days of the new moon's birth, as well as during the late winter and early spring. It is the time when you bleed and the days leading up to ovulation, if these rhythms fit your biology. It is those days when you revel in a sensual sort of aloneness. The Dark Moon Maiden is a woman reborn, and she surrenders to her need for silence and isolation. If you have irregular cycles or do not bleed, you still embody this particular She-Magick around the new moon. If you have a regular cycle but do not bleed around the new moon typically, sleep in total darkness for a time to see if your cycle will regulate according to the lunar rhythms.

The Dark Moon Maiden is on the verge of wielding generative power but is not yet ready. She moves with purpose, and there is magick in her blood. They have told her she is unclean, but she knows the truth. Her blood is fearsome because it is a visible reflection of the sheer force of womb-power. As the Dark Moon Maiden, my Sister, you are the true commander of the life-death spiral. Your magick at this time has been so denigrated because it is wildly misunderstood. You are whole unto yourself, and a fierce independence emanates from your eyes. The Maiden cannot be manipulated, and her intuition is keener than a cat's night vision.

A woman's inner Maiden hugs closely to her root and sacral chakras; this divinity has a grounded sensuality that is nourished by empowered solitude and soulful inquiry. It is the Maiden who craves nature's nourishment and the touch of rough bark to cheek and warm sand to foot. A woman's Maiden becomes underfed when she is too far removed from the nutrients of soil and water; these feed her deep-red primitive roots and jewel-orange sacral center, respectively. Know the divinity of the Maiden by knowing the holiness in all that feeds the body. Eating hearty food, swaying in sultry movement, balling up fresh snow, and relishing the sensual solace of cool sheets on a sweaty night: These are the temple practices of the Maiden.

Declaration of Independence: The Dark Moon Maiden Vows

The divine whole of the universe lives inside your body's electric field, magick Maiden. You are a creature of the night when the moon is but a silver sliver, and your dreams are harbingers of Spirit. At this time, these vows are yours:

> I am a Maiden of the Dark Moon, and my blood is perfect. My eyes have seen the ghosts who so lovingly haunt me in the dark of night, and I am fearless. Nothing can harm me, for I am shielded by sanguine armor. I am stillness. I am silence. I am a lone wolf moving through shadow. I am discerning, and I am sure. I am the moment the soul leaves the body, and I am the moment it returns. I am at once nothing and everything, and I surrender to the solace of spiritual solitude. This breath, this blood, is mine and mine alone.

As the moon turns from dark to new, the Witch feels a deep wound in her cells; it is a collective remembrance of, and consequent grief over, the denigration of bleeding women in our human community. When you honor your power at this time, dear Sister, you vindicate all those who cannot stand for themselves. Your blood is a battle cry, and, when they told you it was dirty, they lied. Your blood is magick, Dark Moon Maiden. Your blood is pure womb-born perfection.

Women sense the dark moon phase's pending arrival in their moods. We become raw and have no apologies left. Women who force themselves to press on during the dark moon phase will tire themselves out with social proprieties, filling their need for darkness and solitude with too-bright substitutes. This is our Red Tent time, Beauty, and you do well to sink into the blessed darkness with all that you are.

WAXING MOON MOTHER

The Mother of the Waxing Moon may be the aspect of your Goddess nature with which you are most comfortable, my love, for it is the parts of you most accepted by our patriarchal world. In this phase lies the extremes of the Madonna and the Whore, with young girls taught, if not directly, then through regular inundation of media messages, that their worth is bound to their ability to please men and bear children, looking damn good doing it all. When women opt to reject these roles, they may unwittingly feel forced to succumb to a masculine-oriented drive to achieve, pursue, dominate, and win over. This is, of course, not to say that women cannot or should not behave in any specific way. Judith Duerk writes in *Circle of Stones* that "the issue is not whether woman can achieve, but that preoccupation with achievement may deny a descent into her deeper nature which a woman must make to touch her true strengths." A woman cannot identify the Mother phase of the Goddess merely with childbearing; it must be framed as a generative, creative, and intensely feminine aspect of your body, psyche, and spirit whose key attributes are love-born action and alchemical change.

As the moon grows toward fullness, so does the wild woman. She becomes a Priestess of Manifestation, a Warrior-Goddess of change fire, and a fertile, flower-haired beauty who believes in relationship and balanced love. The full moon is akin to the ovulation phase of the menstrual cycle and to the summer season. The energy of creation, prana Shakti, is high. Mind you, the Mother aspect of your Goddess nature need not be, or want to be, for that matter, a bearer of children. She may instead choose to nurture her sacred work or pursue other endeavors that require her hands' devotion. As Mother, you make manifest in the world all that you most authentically value, and you protect it with all that you are. You are a magickal, sensual creatrix, and your She-Magick has been heralded since ancient times.

The inner Mother of every woman is bound neither to the traditional role of Mother nor to what is normally referred to as the childbearing years. Just as the Maiden lives in every woman in the lower chakras, the Mother also lives in every woman in her solar plexus, heart, and throat chakras. The Mother craves generative action, relational alchemy, and truth telling. A woman's inner Mother Goddess needs to engage in sacred work that is founded on the creative power of the Maiden. The Mother, in effect, parents the Maiden by streamlining the raw sensual and creatrix energy of the lower chakras into action and purposeful connection. When the Maiden is dominant and the Mother is weak or absent, a woman may feel she is abuzz with the *power to* create but unable to practically manifest this energy through doing.

Nourish the Mother by channeling your sacred work, whatever it might be, into the wild world by connecting to others. Circle with other women or those who strongly embody feminine energy when, though only when, you feel you must. Speak about your passions, your talents, and your high-fire desires; bring these things to life outside the unbridled Maiden-work, burn through obstacles to your freedom, and be Mother to your own soul's purpose.

Womb-Healing Meditation for the Mother of the Waxing Moon

Inside your womb, Mother Witch, is a profound energetic space where unprocessed emotions, traumas, and memories are tucked away and consciously forgotten. Often as an act of self-preservation, we leave our feminine wounds here in the shadows, but they remain very much physically present, coexisting with all of the juicy life-death-marrow that lives between your hip bones. Your sacral center is your energetic womb, even if a physical womb is not present; it undergoes a detox during the Dark Moon Maiden phase, but very often this blood purification is not enough to remove blockages at the womb center. Your womb is the very origin of creation, the heart of the Shakti-divine, and it is worthy of wound cleansing. When I say wound, mind you, I do not mean your sacred shadowy self that is very much a part of you; I mean, in this instance, parts of you that no longer belong. Conceive of womb clearing as a sort of energetic space clearing, like smudging your bedroom with sage after a soon-to-be-forgotten lover leaves you.

Drop your consciousness down to your womb space, my love, and engage your Witch consciousness. Know this space as your inner temple. Assess the energy; does it feel busy? Stagnant? Fluid? Chaotic? Now imagine yourself in this space, spiraling around the womb walls and beaming diamond-light from your hands. Purge anything here that does not serve you. Rid yourself of those who have gained entry to your womb and taught you difficult lessons. This temple belongs to you, High Priestess, and no one else. You are blameless, and there is nothing now but the present time, in which you are the hands-of-light healer of your own womb-wounds.

Now envision the boundaries of this space as impermeable, with only you positioned to grant or deny entry. This womb-work is hard, my love, for it is an unconscious battle in which you have been engaged since adolescence. Now, brought out of the dark to your cognizant mind, you are weighed down with war weariness. Give yourself permission to rest now. Affirm your womb temple as the sacred origin of creativity and sensuality, and affirm yourself as its keeper.

The womb can be considered a vital gateway through which the wild soul moves between the individual woman and the natural world around her. This holy space is your interconnection, the fertile void from which your emotionality and sensuality arise, both feeding and being nourished by the Earth Herself. The womb of nature is the most sacred circle our world has been given and, for this reason, women are keepers of the wild Mystery.

The Wild Child of Soul Purpose

As a Mother, your soul-warrior energy is very strong within you. Ask yourself what you are nurturing in your life right now; it may be your children, but it may also be career, a new craft or practice, or a new-found wild art. Now try to personify your soul's purpose as if it were a growing child. How do you care for this child? What are its favorite meals, and how do you tend to it? Women are Mothers of many things, for we are always creating something. Right now, the life your soul designed for you is growing larger and louder; mother it when you are called to do so, and honor the fallow times when stillness and listening are far better than strategy and action.

Because our society affirms the Mother phase of the Triple Goddess far more than it does the Maiden or the Crone phase, women are pressured into constantly doing. Mother energy is active and relational, and it holds the potential to cage a woman in a perpetual state of high-fire, many-armed juggling. You need long moments of stillness. You need time away from screens, children, friends, partners, and lovers. You need time away from home, and you need solitude in order to integrate the learning done during the fallows. Be a Mother when you are called to be, and be something else entirely when you are not. Any single label for your wild self is insufficient, Sister, and the between-stage movement has much to teach us.

WISE WOMAN OF THE WANING MOON

If the Waxing Moon Mother holds the greatest amount of power in this imbalanced society of ours, the Wise Woman of the Waning Moon is faced with a challenge most severe. Our elders are not afforded the respect they deserve in our world, and the Wise Crone aspect of your Goddess nature may want to cling to the Mother phase of the cycle, holding tightly to the full-moon, high-energy parts of the self. The Wise Woman phase is one of surrender, psychic connection, peace, and letting go, all feminine actions largely dishonored by our action-oriented, individualistic workaday lives. The Wise Woman knows that the void is coming as sure as the sun will set, and She prepares to go into the cave of the dark moon by banishing all that no longer belongs. This is the She-Magick of autumn and early winter, when the nights are long and the veil is thin. You honor this aspect of your Goddess nature through discernment and nonattachment. Remove all obstacles to your liberation at this time, hooded Crone, for you have lived an entire life in a single cycle of the moon.

A woman's inner Wise Woman lives at her third eye and crown

chakras. She is pure intuition, deep vision, and higher consciousness. The inner Crone becomes gaunt and quiet when you ignore your feminine intuition. She stops speaking when she feels she is not being heard and will poke at a woman's psyche through her dreams if she is not attended to during waking hours. The divinity of the Wise Woman is bound to Her omniscience, for She is, in effect, intimately linked to all points in time and space. A vast and deep sea of knowledge stretches through psychic space, beyond the veil of lower-frequency, in-your-face energies, and the Wise Woman knows well how to swim in these salty depths. Attend to Her by showing Her you are listening. Receive gracefully the treasures She brings back for you, and She will gift you with the most abundant and holy riches.

Wise Witch, Burn It to the Ground!

Elder Sister, now is the time to reject all that was necessary in your earlier stages but no longer belongs to you. Now is the time to burn the parts of your life that are not *for you* to the mother-loving ground. This is your late autumn, your waning moon, and the days before your blood comes; it is all of these at once, and every grandmother that has ever lived is inside you right now, in this moment. Lie prostrate on the cold ground near your fire and bow to your own lined face and deep wisdom. Feel the She-Magick writhing around your spine from womb to third eye. Scrawl the words that hold you back on soft wood: *I am too old, I am past my prime, I do not have enough.* Now, my love, cast these falsities into the fire and watch them burn, for you are the Great Goddess of All Things. Nothing can hold you back, for every part of this world belongs to you, as you do to it.

Wisest Witch, you have learned much during these days, months, and years, but time is but a spiral within a spiral. The greatest gift you can give to our wounded world is to be the discerning craftswoman of your own life, and any blockage to that destiny deserves to be burned to ashes. The height of your She-Magick is the ability to create the life you truly desire for yourself, giving yourself permission to be precisely what they told you not to be.

So damning is the perception that a dream is meant to be singularly pursued and achieved, with a permanent plateau of happiness being reached, discounting the need for any future changes. Our life paths are swelling and shrinking organisms, fed quite unpredictably by the great inhales of relationships gained and dreams met, the natural exhales of release and wandering, and moments of breathless pause while the ego reconfigures itself after some significant unlearning. Look to the letting go regularly and often. Look to your life as an ever-changing epic myth that breathes meaning into itself over and over again, with every plot twist and new character an unexpected opportunity for self-inquiry.

The Intuition of the Fallowed Time

The waning moon illuminates the very tip of your crystal third eye like no other lunar phase. Your intuition is heightened now, and your ability to see in the dark is honed. Imagine now that the path of your life is winding through a knotted, overgrown forest where the night creatures walk. The only light you have is the sliver of pale moonlight coupled with the diamond spark at your third-eye center; together, these have made you fearless. Walk this path now with fierce foresight. When the thick of the shadows becomes too overpowering, halt your steps and stand in stillness until clear edges emerge; this is the work of your inner Wise Woman. She knows when to press on actively and when to stand frozen in keen receptivity. Show your inner Crone that you are listening, and she will show you a dark, fertile world normally obscured by the too-bright light of day.

Verses of the Holy Feminine
The Crone's Hymn

———◆———

My age in this life matters not, for my soul is ancient. I
bow low now to my inner Wise Woman who has shown

me a new way to live. By her grace, I can see in the dark, and my many eyes look ever forward without sacrificing fierce presence. I am here, and I am staying. My skin is green with Gaia's loam, my teeth are sharp, and those who do not care to know me will think me fearsome.

I am a hooded sylph crouching with folded wings in a mist of indigo dream-light.

I am a wire-haired bone collector come to claim my dead.

I sing out to the flying raptors and slithering serpents, for these creatures move the way I move. I have resurrected the holy Witch healer who lay so long with hands crossed at heart center, buried deep in the hallows between my ribs. My wise one has awakened, and her lined face looks back at me in the mirror every morning.

I am a soft-skinned selkie sunning myself on the salt-stained rocks.

I am the one who knows, the magick maker.

I will scratch the holy verses onto every surface I find, for she speaks through me now. When my work is finished and my hands are raw, I will rest nestled by her hearth, drunk on burning sage and honey mead. I have taken the Crone as a lover, and now I know I am ever loved.

I am She who is and will always be.

I am the wise elder of the wounded world.

Spirals within Spirals

Time is nonlinear, and your inner Goddess-Witch knows this within her chakral energy centers; they spin clockwise in spirals of reception and offering, being and doing, and surrender and desire. The smallest spiral of time is the lunar cycle, the monthly movement from Maiden to

Mother to Crone, but consider that you move in this wave even within a single breath, with the dark of the moon pervading the breathlessness at the bottom of the exhale before the waxing inhale, peak of breath at the full moon and waning moon as the breath leaves you. The yearly spiral of time is spring's great inhalation, with the breath's peak during the summer months and autumn being nature's out-breath before the breathlessness of winter. As a woman, you are attuned to these spirals of time acutely and intimately, and linear time feels oppressive at best. You know in your Witch's blood that you are more than the socially acceptable role of Mother, more than a potential or actual bearer of children; you are the whole of the birth-death-birth cycle. You are not just a Maiden preparing for motherhood or a Crone who waits for death; you are and have always been feminine complexity embodied in spirals within spirals, swirling rhythmically in line with the natural world. You have been born a Woman Most Wild, and the divine Witch is alive within your blood.

Chapter 4

Hallowed Yoga
and Your Energy Alchemy

A Witch's body, and by extension her sensuality, is inseparable from her spirituality. Knowing your magickal body as a confluence of energetic vibrations is as integral to spiritual practice as knowing how to pray or meditate. Within your subtle body exists seven primary centers of energy, your chakral wheels of light and dark, and they relate to all aspects of your being. Your chakras, when balanced, receive and gift energies that reflect and nourish who you are. Both the solar and lunar rhythms affect the chakras in profound, and unfortunately often ignored, ways, with the relationship between the sun, the moon, and your chakral system a beauteous symbiotic trinity. This chapter asks that you, my Sister-Witch, consider your being as an intricately woven fabric of vibrating, subtle energies and more static, denser, visible parts. Know your cells, bones, organs, and muscles as tiny God-Goddess-spells; they are places of both action and reception, and they are marked by divinity.

Yoga, in its most authentic and practical definition, is a process of finding and removing any obstacles to the liberation of your spirit and soul; while physical movement alchemy is an integral part of yoga practice, it is far from the crux of the work. Yoga, as it is commonly practiced in Western society, is a pale reflection of its spirit-centered, original incarnation. The roots of yoga, uncovered in the ancient Indus-Saraswati civilization, sourced nourishment from the ethereal in order to drive personal transformation. The Witch knows her yoga as a deeply challenging and ongoing process of delving into her depths, harvesting wounds, digging out unprocessed emotions, and, in short, doing the work of soul as much as that of spirit. Spirit calls you toward objectivity and connection, while soul calls you toward the subjective experience of being most authentically you. Spirit is why we are all here, but soul is why *you* are here. The Witch's yoga is a practice of moving through shadow as much as through light, and many of these shadows are harbored in the lower chakras, your soul's moonlit home.

We have learned to make damn sure that our sensuality and our spirituality sleep in separate beds, but know that the Tantric union of body and spirit is a practice that will support you through myriad channels. The woman who nourishes her body through regular cycles of movement, consumption of nutritious foods, and sacred sexuality is a woman who attends to her lower soul-centered chakras. The woman who attends to her creative, generative, and sacred work through action and conscious connection is a woman who attends to her middle, ego, heart, and throat chakras, just as the woman who affords attention to spirit by engaging her intuition and deep wisdom has upheld her own spiritual essence and growth. The woman who regularly supports whole-being integration of body, mind, and spirit, however, is a wild woman who has become an alchemical agent of the sacred self.

THE WITCH'S SOUL CHAKRAS

Harbor a healthy skepticism of any tea, oil, or impersonalized treatment that promises to balance your chakral system; there is no one-size-fits-all magick that suits everyone's strengths and weaknesses. Moreover, remember that your chakras are soul-designed for you to live the purpose that is yours. If a wound exists, for instance, at your heart's center, consider that experiencing that wound — be it betrayal, abandonment, or loss — is a pivotal point on your destined path. True healing, then, is an act of clearly seeing into your depths rather than trying to fix or, worse, bury, these wounds. Become a seeker of soul by the light of the moon, magickal Yogini, and then you will truly begin to know yourself.

Inside your lower three chakras — namely Muladhara, Svadhisthana, and Manipura — lives your individuality. Finding obstacles to your soul's freedom demands examining what lies beneath, with the gifts of these chakras serving to shape your very identity. Muladhara, your root chakra, vibrates at the base of your spine. Physically, your root is your bones and your bowels, these deep and primal aspects of self that are heavy and material. Your most tightly gripped beliefs about home, money, health, and the natural world are harbored here at your root, my love, either feeding or starving all other chakras from below to varying degrees. At your womb-center lies Svadhisthana, the ripe center of all things sensual, sexual, and emotional. If your root is Earth, your sacral center is water; it is changeable, spontaneous, creative, and juicy, embodying all beliefs about your She-Magick and feminine, Shakti powers. The heat of transformation then emanates from your belly flame, Yogini-Sister, with Manipura fueling your action and your will. Inside your solar plexus burn all your beliefs about your individuality, your right to effect change in your life and in that of others; it is your *tapas,* your purifying fire, and it is your resistance to surrender.

A woman's lower three chakras form the foundation for communion and relationship. At the soul level, she roots down into the wild world as the Maiden before connecting deeply to it as the Mother and Wise Woman. Learn the language of the outer rainbow, the warm and soulful reds, oranges, and yellows, and you will begin to truly speak in the mother tongue of Soul.

The Language of the Outer Rainbow:
Communing in Red, Orange, and Yellow

Even the Witch is very much accustomed to listening to the voices of her thinking mind over those of the soul. Your thoughts are loud, my love, and the whispers of your lower body are often drowned out by the screams of future hopes and past regrets. Tune in to the language of your lower chakras, and you will hear the voice of your true self. Now, Witch, gather your materials and ready yourself for deep listening.

Go into a secret garden, a place where you can be one with nature, if you are able. Lean your back against a tree most holy, and drop your consciousness down, down, and down farther still. Alternatively, go into your home's wild sanctuary and lean against a wall, envisioning the presence and support of a tree in as much detail as possible. Feel where your pelvic floor and Gaia's ground meet, for here, at this point of contact, you can hear Her heart beating. Close your eyes now, and envision the colors and shapes of the root; know that your Muladhara may not be red and beauteous. How does the energy move there at the base of your spine? Does it swirl in slow spirals? Does it lay stagnant? How big does the root feel? Now, my love, on your exhale pull this root energy up through the chakras of the soul to the bridge of the heart; once there, let that primal Earthly energy flood down your arms and into your palms. When ready, let the root speak! Either freewrite in a journal, or vocalize all that your base chakra wants to tell you in this moment. Know that it may be much or little, it may be succinct or ambiguous; the words of your root may come easily or with much difficulty. Once the root has spoken, visually depict this magickal chakra with paint on canvas, pastel on paper, or colored sand on ground. Offer gratitude to your root for communing with you, and move your consciousness up to the seat of your womb.

Here between your hip bones vibrates a formidable energy of both light and shadow. What colors move there at your sacral center, and how fluidly does the energy move? Does the sacral center seem to be fed from the root below? Is your energetic womb well nourished and well grounded? Pull the sacral energy up to your heart center and, when ready, let the sacral energy speak to you. What does it tell you? Svadhisthana may tell you of deeply seated wounds or fears, memories you believed to be resolved fully, or dreams of womb-healing. Whatever it may say, listen to your sacral center with all that you are, for it is the very marrow of your feminine power. My love, the words of your womb may well make you weep, for all collective women's wounds reside there. Give your womb permission to speak, and honor its wisdom, for this is the voice of the Goddess Herself. Create your womb as a visual work of art now, a truly profound process, placing it just above your root on whatever base you were using.

Finally, shift your Witch's consciousness to your belly, and attune to the fiery energy. What colors are in those flames? What shapes? What images? How is the energy moving? Erratically like a bonfire, slow and rhythmic like a burning Yule log, or dying and hissing like a campfire in the rain? Pull this heated energy up just a little higher to your heart, and let it speak it to you. How loud is the voice of Manipura? Does it seem aggressive or weak? What words does it have for you about your sacred work, self-esteem, or soul's purpose? Now, do this magick chakra justice by reflecting its beauty visually, in your medium of choice, placing it just above your sacral chakra.

Look at your chakral art now, seeing these three soulful energies as they showed themselves to you. Title your work, Witch. What shall you call this reflection of your innermost being? As a whole, what feelings do these chakras invoke in you? Now bless this work like the Priestess you are, and let the Earth Mother bless it from below.

Visually representing your chakral system is a powerful practice of body attunement. The very acknowledgment of your chakras as inextricably bound to aspects of both the physical and the numinous is an act of binding body to spirit. Wild woman spirituality begs you to consciously forge meaningful connections between all aspects of your vital being; do this in small ways, by simply feeling an emotion in your body, and through more involved but still accessible practices of whole-body ritual. Pray with your body, and dance with your spirit. Sing hymns of your sacred sexuality, and meditate on your wild worth.

Earth, Water, Fire!
A Nontraditional Yoga Practice for the Witch's Soul

It's time to beat the drums and run wild, too-tamed Yogini! Leave the mat at the studio, for that rectangle of rubber will not serve you today. The raw ground will be your practice space. Now stomp your bare feet and know yourself as a Lady of the Unnamed Mountain. Root yourself down into the Earth by lifting all your toes and digging the bony parts of the feet into the mud. Draw the Gaia energy up through your legs, lifting and lengthening the muscles. Let it find your pelvis now, and lift the pelvic floor straight up to your heart. Lift the deep belly, invigorating your soul's physical seat and feeding the heart. In this shape, my wise sage, you have truly found the Earth.

Now, watery Witch, begin to let your Shakti snake slither and shake, moving your hips in sultry swirls. Dance as your inner Maiden dances, unbridled and with all the sensuality of a waxing spring moon. Drink in the scent of your forbidden nature, and let your breath guide your movement. Stick out your tongue. Exhale open-mouthed. Stretch your arms high, and thrust your pelvis forward. Swing your arms deep and low, folding to the ground. Let the water take you and shake you, and know your feminine juices as lunar nectar.

The belly fire has been lit. You are Goddess of the Burning Flame; now run! Circle the trees, and let nothing contain you. You are a Yogini liberated from notions of perfect alignment. Feel the beat of your heart-drum in your chest, and surrender to nothing. Woman, you are *tapas* embodied, and every desire you have will come to pass through this ferocious alchemy. Know it to be true! You are an elemental Witch of earth, water, and fire! Your mind will tire long before your body begins to weaken, but, when you are ready, sink to the ground and let Her feed you. Wild Witch, this was a yoga practice most true. These elements of soul live inside your perfect body, from the depths of the Earth to the depths of the Witch. The light and darkness within my Witch's soul honors that in you.

Awaken to the wild through movement, and you will fuse a long-lost partnership between sex and spirit. By sex, I mean the slick, sensual marrow of sweet, juice-filled presence, and by spirit, I mean the essential and universal connection between all things. Women long to feel full and ripe in their sexuality, but such feelings are associated with the loss of control, shameful and forbidden behavior, and, perhaps most salient, the potential for rejection. Yoga holds the power to remove these deeply seated blockages to your sensual freedom. Shiva Rea writes, in *Tending the Heart-Fire*, that "within Tantra, the cosmology of the universe and the rhythms of the Earth are all directly mirrored in the body." From a Tantric perspective, the body is divine, and all women are the embodiments of the sacred feminine. Take time to move unabashedly and only in your own presence, examine any voice that arises from within quite objectively, and begin a regular and raw yoga practice that holds the sensual as holy.

Every woman's soul is unique, and consequently, few generalizations can be made about the chakral system that will suit every woman equally. Similarly, the relationship between your personal, pranic vibrations and those of the lunar cycles will not precisely mirror that of any other being. The following descriptions are intended to be accessible guidelines for how women commonly receive and adapt to the moons of the year, but know that there are multiple and unforeseen influences at work within our lives. The magick of the Mystery is that we can self-examine, understand our inner and outer cycles, and still be endlessly curious about and open to what comes.

Your Root Chakra and the Moons of Winter

Your root chakra is your oldest chakra, and you have harbored this magick since you were in the womb. Inside your root lies your impulse to survive, to have your most fundamental needs met, and to feel safe in our world. You have a natural inclination toward root nourishment during the winter months, Snow Priestess of the Wolves, and the moons of winter call you toward your den. While the outside world is making many demands on you, your very nature charges you to go inward, to find soul-food in solitude, and to sink your roots strong and deep. The winter season, however, can be framed as two relatively distinct periods of time, with early winter still bound to the inner Crone and late winter a time of Maiden awakening. Your Wise Woman ways ground you in sacred silence, secure stillness, and deep knowing, but your Maiden craves physicality and bodily nourishment.

A balanced root chakra during the winter months feels secure, fed, and healthy. An energetic imbalance at the root may deplete your entire chakral system, manifesting in a blocked root that is either laden with too much or starving from too little nourishment. Our primitive nature demands that we afford attention to our root as the snow falls, causing us to overeat and overspend. In essence, it is human to try to counter our fears of scarcity during the winter season by gathering fiercely. The material things you gather and the foods you eat are very basic ways to create your Witch's winter nest. By extension, the greatest self-care you can do at this time is to healthily address the fear of not having enough. The moons of December, January, and February are mystical, lunar rhythms that live inside your Witch's soul, just as a stealthy and discerning wolf mother lives inside her den.

The Moons of the Long Night, the Wolf, and the Quickening: A Fragile Essence

The first moon of winter, the Long Night's Moon, aligns with the solar energies of the winter solstice; it is a moon of sacred gift giving, nurturing family, and celebration. Too often the early winter season is a time of energetic depletion and Witch's exhaustion. As women, we offer much of ourselves to our loved ones at a time when our own roots demand to be nourished most. Practices of self-care must be fierce at this time of year, and you must give yourself full permission to check out when your soul and spirit are drained. As this first winter moon waxes, there is an intimate connection between the higher-frequency chakras, or the realm of your inner Wise Woman, and the root, or the realm of the Maiden. Fuse your intuitive nature with your physical needs while the nights are long, and you will learn to see with night vision.

The Wolf Moon, marking the second lunar cycle of winter, highlights your wild intuition. The dawn of a new solar year may weigh on you like a thousand-tonned boulder, my love, for the world is telling you to throw yourself full force back into the frenzied swing of activity. In your bones you know that this second winter moon has not risen to aid you in the creation of vision boards or a new exercise plan; instead, it begs you to listen with the ears of a wolf mother. Be a receptor rather than a beacon at this time, keenly observing with all your senses but holding tight to your own energy for now. During this midwinter time your inner Maiden begins to stir, and your instincts are alive and awake, though your physical energy may still be slow moving.

Generally the last moon of the winter season, the Quickening Moon, follows the solar energies of Imbolc, the midway point between winter solstice and the vernal equinox; it is a time of immense, often manic, inspiration. The Maiden is fully awake now, and your root and sacral chakras are craving vital nourishment. The impulse to create is overwhelming as the seeds begin to spark to life underground. You feel the fires of Imbolc deep in your Witch's belly, and you are torn between surrendering to these flames completely or soothing them through some rooted manifestation. Channel your creativity at this time, my love, for the dawning of the sensual season is upon you.

The woman in winter experiences much transition as she moves from the early winter season's time of rest and rejuvenation to the late season's demand for action; it is akin to the shift that occurs as the moon goes dark and then sparks to light. She may move from a sense of nothingness toward a sense of great purpose, and she does this in a matter of weeks. The wild woman honors her needs at this time with no expectation of any particular outcome or success; the goal is simply to intuit, nourish, and *be*. The connection between the root and the sacral chakra is born of liberation, with a woman necessarily taking the soul-gifted resources she has and organizing them with much creative spunk and raw risk taking.

Your Sacral Chakra and the Moons of Spring

At your sacral center dances your inner Maiden, and she is most awake in the spring. All your experiences and beliefs about sensuality, change, creation, and fertility spiral around in your womb-heart. The Witch in spring may be seen as irresponsible in her fierce presence, for she has no time for foresight or strategy. She wants to feel. In the spring your sensual Maiden is fueled by the same pranic spark of life that calls the seeds to sprout and the flowers to bloom. There is passion in the air, and you, Witch, can feel it in your bones. Your linear age matters not, for you are pure She-Magick under the moons of spring, no matter what year you were born.

Your sacral chakra is akin to the water element, and it is ideally balanced in a fluid, flexible state. Womb-woundings can easily prompt rigidity at your sacral center, however, turning what is meant to flow easily into static ice. Other woundings can prompt the waters of Svadhisthana to run uncontrolled as if the floodgates have been opened, gushing untamed sexual and emotional outpourings anywhere and everywhere. Warm and channel the sacral energy in the spring, Witch, and you will wield the power of natural magick.

A woman in spring is a woman off the nest and in the world. She experiences a total surrendering to nature's orgasmic eruption of color, scent, and sound and becomes unapologetically re-wilded as the green things sprout underfoot. Spring is a time of purpose and action, unlike winter, and the air is laden with the heavy wet of nature's love juices.

The Moons of the Storm, the Hawk, and the Budding Trees: Engaging Renewal

The first moon of spring hardly holds the quiet innocence of a newborn lamb; rather, it embodies the passionate and unbridled ferocity of an ocean before a storm. The energies of the vernal equinox are those of life's budding potential, and the world outside your window buzzes with the electricity of birth. The Storm Moon calls you to tie yourself to the mast. Let this spring weather toss you about. Be windswept, and have no expectations. Your sacral chakra, when balanced, welcomes these natural, high-energy, flourishing times just as it does the fallow quiet in our lives; it is adaptable to change, for it embodies the quality of fluidity.

At midspring, the storm begins to calm, leaving behind clearer skies and begging you to look forward with much scrutiny. The Hawk Moon's essence follows the storm; it holds a fierce knowing that spaces have been opened up for creative work, planning, and manifestation. Consider this moon one of introspection and careful discernment, as if the new moon were dawning just after a raging thunderstorm has passed. Look to the world as it is now, having been tossed about and purified with rain. Any decisions are made from this vantage point, and you see the world with objective but all-seeing eyes that lead the coming march forward.

As the cusp of summer approaches, the Witch sinks deep into a time of high manifestation. While your inner winter Crone begged you to wait and watch, your swelling spring Maiden-Mother now demands that you stand and claim what is yours. These life-giving energies live within you just as they live in the teeming woodland or watery depths. This Budding Trees Moon, the last of the lunar spring rhythms, finds you on the cusp of fruition, and a woman at this time may seek intimacy, in its myriad forms, more often than usual.

Know that the precipice of summer is often fearsome, with women looking out on their lives as if a wildfire were threatening all they know to be true. The flames are moving closer, and though she has herself set the blaze, she may be reluctant to see her world catch fire. A wild woman honors the natural trepidation of summer's heat, and she learns to accept the changes born of her own desires and sacred purpose, be they initially welcome or not. The bridge between the sacral and solar plexus chakra is built from dynamic, alchemical shifts, with the woman integrating the emotionality, sensuality, and creativity that is wholly *hers* and potentially hidden into outward, very visible action.

Your Fire Chakra and the Moons of Summer

Summer and early autumn are very telling times, and you are a Goddess of Transformation. As the days grow thick with heat and swelter, your belly fire burns bright. The moons of summer call you to further authenticate your identity; if you are playing a role that no longer aligns with your soul's truth, these moons will eclipse those outmoded ways of being from your world. If winter is a time for careful introspection and examination, then spring is a time for fertile manifestation of what your soul desires most. Summer is then a time for great revelry; it is an enduring time of those weeks after giving birth when the mother cares for nothing more than nourishing her newborn. Lead with your soft belly during these months, summer Witch, for with autumn comes the great exhale.

Your Manipura chakra is where your instincts, ego, and sense of self are centered; here you act to carry your talents, skills, and passions into the world. Mind you, it is possible for the fire to burn too brightly at your belly center, leading to aggression and arrogance. Just the same, your belly fire may well be too dim, and with a weakened inner flame comes the notion that actions do not have consequences. Ask yourself this, Witch: Do you believe that your soul has the divinely ordained right to effect change in this world? Revel in all that spring has given you now, and know that when you gift your purpose to the world, you are fueling holy, global transformation. Do not discount yourself, for the world needs your bright torch.

The energies of the Mother are outward and active, with the summer season similarly made manifest in a woman's life. A sense of natural selfishness arises during this high-fire season, and a normally responsible woman may break promises and relinquish obligations. A balance comes from honoring the needs of the self as well as those of her world. She speaks only what is true, she honors the integrity of the relationships that feed her, and she burns away all else.

The Moons of the Strong Sun, Blessing, and Corn: Gratitude and Blissful Union

With the Strong Sun Moon, the first moon of summer, comes a sense of immoderation. The whole of nature bursts with ecstatic color, and you can barely contain yourself. Under this moon, you are unapologetically you in whatever situation you find yourself. You revel in your passions, all the while taking stock of the beautiful life you designed for yourself.

The Strong Sun Moon is the moon of the unapologetic, shining self. This is the time of complete fruition and whole-being presence.

The hedonistic moon bath of the solstice breeds gratitude under the second summer moon as your heart chakra asks to be nourished. In this season of enjoyment and revelry, be grateful for the abundance you have been gifted. Know that the Witch's currency holds the value of magick, sisterhood, and nature's blessings, and this July moon is a time to give thanks. The Blessing Moon tells you of your abundance, and you are called to actively appreciate all that you value in preparation for the coming harvest of late summer.

With the season's looming end comes a deeper understanding of the waning moon cycle. Summer is the season of fullness and fruition, and autumn a time of release. The Corn Moon's energies ask you to enjoy the last of the warm nights with all that you are. Be present, and, as much as possible, resist the urge to look forward and prepare for all that you are to be blown away on a cool autumn wind.

The moons of summer are those of abundance and grace, and the cycle of the fire season contains a majestic magick. Your lower three soul chakras live out their individual gifts, passions, and woundings in the winter, spring, and summer seasons; this is not to say that your upper chakras are in any way dormant for three-quarters of the year, but rather that the particular qualities of the autumn speak loudly to your upper chakras, with the Mother and Wise Woman particularly engaged at this time.

YOUR HIGHER CHAKRAS AND THE MOONS OF AUTUMN

As the days grow colder, your Witch's soul is most at home. She revels in this time of magick and change, with the thinned veil revealing a fertile world of Spirit that complements the materiality of Soul. You have been the wise Crone in early winter, sinking Her roots deep into ground, the dancing Maiden in late winter and early spring bathing in sacral waters, and the voluptuous Mother in summer reveling by the fire. Now, my love, move away from the foundations of your soul-ground toward the higher plane of spirit.

Just above your solar plexus vibrates the emerald green of Anahata, the heart-bridge between the individual and divinity. The heart chakra is a Mother chakra, and its energies are prone to expansion during late summer and early autumn. Your heart-brain vibrates with the frequency of compassion and empathy; it is the resonance of healing hands and the Earth's electromagnetic field. All the gifts your soul has designed for you affect relationship and community here in the heart-light, further shaping the landscape of your wild life. At throat center, the story of your Witch's heart will be told, carried out through your strong voice and individual myth. You, Heroine, ascend under the moons of autumn to your role as a change agent. What story do you want to be told when your death rites are given? What is your legacy? Under the autumn moons, all that is not you will be cut away, and you will be left with a clear third eye–born vision of who you truly are. At your violet spirit crown vibrates your enduring universal connection to all things, and the Ethereal Witch is awakened to higher purpose when the winds of change blow away all that is dead.

The Moons of Harvest, Blood, and Ancestors: Welcoming the Reaper to Bed

The new Harvest Moon shines its pink-orange light on your open palms as you begin to release your grip on who you used to be, before the summer sun burned your outmoded roles to ash. All three of the autumn moons engage our feminine need for release and darkness. The heart and throat chakras' relationship to the solar plexus was set aflame during the summer months as your inner Mother carried her creative work into the world. Now, under the Harvest Moon, the heart and throat nourish the third eye's vision and crown's wisdom. The high-frequency spaciousness of the autumn moons speaks to the Gypsy in every woman, and this unique wanderlust is inextricably bound to the knowledge that death awaits us around every dark corner.

As the Blood Moon waxes, women tend to feel a slight twinge of melancholy. The veil is reaching its thinnest point, and it seems that ghosts, actual or metaphorical, pervade the natural world. There is a strong focus on the third eye at this time for wild women as they begin to see beings of the ether that were hidden during the other seasons by light and life. During early autumn more than at any other time of year, my love, be kind to yourself as you move through significant internal changes. You may feel you are undergoing an intense and rapid maturation as your inner Wise Elder takes over. You may feel less connected to your body than you do at other times of the year, and you are called to give a nod to every divine wink that comes your way.

The Ancestors Moon serves as a remedy to the longing born from the Blood Moon, with women called to honor those who have passed over to Spirit through ritual and remembrance. Engage the third eye with an intuitive understanding that those whom you have lost remain around you, holding your hand, waiting for your time to come. Consider the ancestors you have not known in this life as ghostly cheerleaders for your soul-work, and relish this late autumn time as the yearly Witching hour.

The Thirteenth Moon: A Divined Vision of Your Witch's Crown

Sister, you are a God-Star. At your crown chakra vibrates the high-frequency energy of divinity; here your divine right as the Goddess embodied is most deeply embedded. Under the Thirteenth Moon of late autumn, the world has sunk into a void of Mystery and not-knowing. You hold both the innocence of a child and the wealthy wisdom of an aged medicine woman. This is a time for honoring your highest self, your enduring spirit, that which will remain long after your body's spark has gone out. The light of your Witch-Spirit is everlasting, my love, and were you to see it, you would weep at its perfection. Wear your Witch's crown with pride, royal Sister, for I bow to you. Know your violet crown as extending out in all directions, effortlessly and with celestial arms, for it is your birthright to know yourself as God-Goddess-Divine.

At the Thirteenth Moon of the year, a woman is most deeply connected to spirit. She sees the Holy Wild in all things, including herself, and she may move through the world with a sense of weightlessness, knowing she is on the cusp of the longest night. She may feel, at this time more than ever, that there are no rules for her body or psyche that she does not make herself. It is as if the power has gone out inside the bright room of ego, and spirit is allowed to move as it will. Be wild in the dark, wise Sister, for the wheel continues to turn.

Verses of the Holy Feminine
Body-Love Letter to the Rising Witch

Her soft majestic body is a holy land, and, to the rising Witch, this love letter is my sacred offering:

From out of the infertile soil of oppression, the Witch is rising. Blessed be her deep, ruddy roots, for they seek out the natural nutrients of the wild world and keep her bare feet firm on hallowed ground. She is the heirloom seed planted under the full moon. She is the branch stretching skyward. She is the most ancient tree and the brightest, impermanent flower.

From out of the media-sustained swamp of body shame, the Witch is rising. Blessed be her jewel-orange sacral center, for it writhes and wriggles with all the passion of the She-Snake. She is soft-bodied self-worth. She is the guiltless consummation of her soul marriage. She is an open-legged body prayer and a howl moonward.

From the crucible of soul-mandated transformation, the Witch is rising. Blessed be her belly flame; it is a funeral pyre for who she used to be and a burning birthing bed for who she will become. She is fearless sacrifice. She is purposed passion. She is the stellar fusion of all she used to be and all she desires.

From out of her dark night of the unruined soul, the

Witch is rising. Blessed be her emerald heart, for with all its wounded memories, surely it remains whole. She is a night spent weeping and the dawn of solitude. She is Lilith's choice to leave Eden. She is sacred vulnerability and compassionate connection in the face of adversity.

From out of the psychic shadows where secrets abound, the Witch is rising. Blessed be her bright-blue voice, for it resonates with the holy truth. She is a refusal to stay quiet, and she is her birthright to speak and be heard. She is maternal lullaby and death-metal ire.

From out of the ethereal realm of spirit, the Witch is rising. Blessed be her indigo eye, as it opens to a feminine future and closes to shame. She is foresight. She is divination. She is the Crone's intuition and the Maiden's instinct.

From out of the greatest Mystery, the Witch is rising. Blessed be her violet, far-reaching crown, connecting her to the wild cosmic infinite and naming her High Priestess. She is the deified woman. She is a rewritten holy book and the vindicated Mother of Babylon. She is the feminine spark immanent in all. She is you, and she is rising. She is me, and she is rising. From out of our wounded world, the Witch is rising.

THE TURNING OF THE FIRST KEY
AND AWAKENING TO RITUAL

All your chakras are alive with energy at any given moment, but each of the four solar seasons speaks through some of our vibrantly colored energy centers more loudly than others. In many ways, our solar year can be framed as a metaphor for our chakral relationships and the internalization of the Triple Goddess archetype. Be kind to yourself now as knowledge of how the rhythms of nature live within you catalyzes a shift in perception. You may begin a process of psychic reorganization, ordering your memories of the solar and lunar cycles as experiences of your truest self.

You have learned nothing new, for you have always known of the Maiden's bliss at late winter and spring as the moon waxes, the fertile Mother's fruition in summer at the lunar peak, and the Crone-like wisdom of autumn and early winter. These rhythms are your gifts, blessed Witch, and a life lived in accordance with these rhythms is one whose foundation has been poured with the very blood-essence of the cosmos. The bones of our social structures are hard and masculine, but the marrow, my love, the juicy *marrow* is feminine. The bones have forgotten what lives and breathes inside them — the Maiden's sensuality, the Mother's generative creativity, and the Wise Woman's intuitive knowing — but harvest the marrow, Sister, for you truly are a Woman Most Wild.

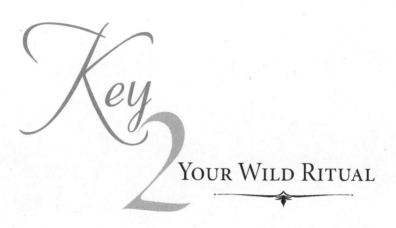

Key 2
Your Wild Ritual

✦ Invocation

I recognized the Wild One, and then She saw me, too.

We waited for the dark to run, and now we come for you.

Meet us on the wild hill where we will light the fires

And burn to ash the ties to will with ripe and raw desires.

We are wild and have come home to see magick in the night.

We are wild and now we roam in darkness and in light.

Unchained we are, and free we'll stay, so shed your armored skin.

We are women, come what may, and wild we've always been.

*F*ix your gaze on the single open lock, dear Sister. Nestle into your deep knowing of how all natural rhythms beyond this door ebb and flow inside your being, spiraling through your chakral system as life-giving, soul-feeding prana. I am giving you permission to drink the tea of knowledge and eat the fruit that has been forbidden for so long. You now know yourself not only as Maiden, Mother, and Crone; you know yourself as nature's divine-born She-Magick that is ever-evolving, ever-free.

Hold the second key tightly now. Notice how it glitters and turns of its own volition in the palm of your hand. This is the Key of Wild Ritual, and it holds much power. Recall the transitions of your life, both celebrated and solemn: birthdays, holidays, unions, and blessed partings. Call to mind the sense of importance, culture, and ceremony that gave meaning to these events. Rites of passage were marked with poetic words, the gathering of friends and family, gift giving, and high emotion. These, my love, are the magnificent rituals of your people.

Now recall the times in your life when you knew, really knew, that magick existed in the world. By magick, I mean both the mysterious interconnectivity of the cosmic web that permits alchemical changes in the human community *and* the outcome of your own agency in creating shifts in your world. In the hands of the Witch, magick is a powerful complement to your cyclical nature. While your wild rhythm, to a certain extent, demands that you surrender to the relationship between your being and the natural world, your wild ritual grants you an immense amount of power born from your will.

The feminine's ability to make use of its magick is an undeniable change agent in our wounded world. The second pillar of wild woman spirituality is the agency of the Witch to enact her magick for the good of all; this means rejecting the notion that magick is a selfish tool for manipulating the energetic field solely for personal gain. While the Witch uses magick and ritual to carefully craft the boundaries around her own life, to color her world with the bright hues of her own daydreams, she also uses her magick to drive positive changes in the global community. The reclamation of the Witch's role as a healer will be born from women's use of magick to craft positive transformations in the world around them. In essence, a woman who heals herself also heals the world, with magick a perfectly positioned and organically powerful tool that can be wielded for such healing.

A woman who feels drained from day-to-day tasks, necessary as they may be, may feel she is hardly an energetic source of power. Moreover, she may look to this particular pillar of her spirituality as burdensome, as if it is another thing to do among a slew of have-tos. She may resist the call to magick just as she may reject herself as a natural creatrix. Women often say they are "not creative," which really means they have been told at some point that their creativity will not be fruitful, that it was not perfect enough, that they did not stay inside the lines, that they would never be able to make a living with their sweet singing, sultry cooking, or whatever their medium may be. Women are natural magick makers because of the inherently generative power they hold in their wombs. Look to your ritual and your spellcraft as energy raising, not energy depleting, and, most salient, consider your ability to work magick both as an innate talent that you may have been underusing and as a learned skill that can be honed.

The promise of the second key is this: As a wild woman, your authentic ritual is fed by a collective culture of natural magick and feminine power. Do not feel, not for one second, that you are unworthy or incapable. Consider yourself a High Priestess in your own temple of the wild woman. You need nothing external, for the power of She-Medicine lies within your Witch's soul. The voice bidding you to embrace ritual and magick is inborn, my love, so insert the second key in the lock and listen to your own heart's command.

Chapter 5

Circle-Casting
and Your Wild Ecology

*C*ircles are a sacred shape inherent to the wild feminine. Your body knows no hard edges or sharpened corners; so, too, the circle is a strong, organic, and living *place* in space and time. Consider the magick circle an energetic container for your work that is as much akin to a cell or organ in your physical body as it is to a chakra in your subtle pranic field or, more visibly, a cook pot or fire pit in your outer world. The circle is an ecological position, and it is the Witch's way of affirming to the universe, *I am here.* The circles wild women have cast over time hold the intention for spells and rituals and, even if you have never cast a circle before, you still harbor a deep knowing of circle-casting technology in your Witch's blood. Read now of the directional and elemental essences, dear Sister, and honor yourself as a global Priestess of Place. Know your position on our magick planet, and consider your personal magick as integral not only to the human community but also to the whole of Gaia's queendom.

When you cast a circle, you are not merely going through the motions of acknowledging directions; you are paying tribute to the ways these directions and elements live inside you. You are claiming your birthright as a woman of this world who knows her own magnificence, her right to *be*, and her divine nature. Casting a circle should never be discounted as a mere preliminary step before the work begins, for it is a sacred endeavor in its own right. Each of the directions holds a particular essence, juice, or *rasa*, and the container for spellwork is formed through the wild woman's call for these directions to ground, enliven, energize, and purify the circle.

Women's fast-paced lives often preclude their awareness of whole-being presence. The scatteredness of the multitasking mind is a formidable barrier to a consistent touchstone of awareness that the being is not just the mind but a symbiotic union between body, mind, and spirit. The circle embodies a homing quality that allows the Witch to nestle into the warm arms of pure presence. In the circle, she is here and now. In the circle, there is no division between body, mind, and spirit, for all three sacred parts converge to craft the magick. In the circle, the woman finds true holism and a state of physical awareness that grounds that of her spiritual practice. She declares the directions in relation to where she stands, and in that moment she is the absolute center point of the cosmos.

Your Steadfast Roots
The Witch's North

The North lives in you with all the steadfastness and immutability of an ancient oak's deepest roots. The North is akin to the winter season, the element of Earth, and the most fundamental parts of your being; it is your bones and your bowels, your bare feet buried in cold mud, and the mature, fiercely nurturing Earth Mother. The northern aspect of the circle is defined by strength and ground, and it resonates in your Witch's consciousness as willful resilience and an uncompromising sense of purpose.

A woman needs to feel her own weight; she needs to plant her feet firmly on the ground and sink into the heft of her own body. The northern aspects of the feminine psyche are those bound to hearth, home, nurturing love, and resources. The North is uncompromising and quantifiable in its density; it does not flit about aimlessly with fragile wings but sends its roots deeply into places where the vital subterranean blood runs reliably and without apology. The Witch calls out to the North when she casts her circle as a fierce declaration of unquestionable and authoritative density. She says: I have a right to stand on these two feet *now*, in this moment and in this place — and the North listens.

Blizzard Witch: A Meditation on Certainty

Plant yourself firmly on cold ground now, and stand with certainty as you face the holy North. Point your fingertips toward the Earth, arms at your sides like hardened vines, and raise your chin like the Crone-Goddess you are. This direction holds you as positively doubtless, a woman who is so sure of her place in this world that the structure of her body seems to be built more of rock than of skin and bone. Stand as if you have always been here, in this place, with the seasons and weather of this world writhing around you with naught more influence than a soft breeze. You are unaffected by the elements' attempts to carve and bend you, and you smile, unmoved, as a great blizzard threatens to take you down.

Close your eyes and curl your lips, my love, for this storm does not know the challenge it faces. Do not waver, not one bit, in your position and your purpose, for you hold all the wise, poetic, and nurturing words of our grandmothers inside your roots. Let the frigid winds batter your bare skin, bidding you to freeze and crumble. Let the snow creatures ride the spiraling winds toward you, bearing their jagged teeth and yellow eyes. Grin as the sharp ice pelts your chest and your belly, and trust that your roots are strong. You have weathered far worse than this, Warrior-Priestess, and you will remain strong and stable long after this storm has given way to clear winter sky. Affirm this now, great Keeper of the North: *I am the North. I am the strength of a thousand ancient oaks embodied in one woman. I am every grandmother's grace in the face of danger, and I am whole unto myself.*

Journey to the Palace of Ice: A Conversation with the Hermit Queen

The winds have calmed, dear one, but your hands and feet have gone numb. This journey has been arduous, and you have lost your sense of place. The endless white land extends in all directions, surrounding you in an eternal sphere of frozen landscape; you are not sure where the dull sky begins and where the snow-covered land ends, and your will to continue has weakened.

Screw up your courage now, Witch! You are almost there! Close your eyes and turn your body in a slow circle, finding your true North; you will know when you feel a sense of purpose and clarity at your heart's center. The North inside you will leap toward the magnetic North of this Earth like two halves famished for wholeness, and your sense of certainty will return. Keep trudging North now, for She has been waiting. Mind you, a thousand years to you is but one winter's season to Her, and She cares not whether you make it by the end of this long day.

Dig your boots deep into the frozen stuff, Woman of the White Wolves, and squint until you see the smoke from Her fire. Her home is not what you pictured, the palace of ice more an unassuming cavern of rock and snow, but the quickening of your heart-drum's rhythm tells you that She is there. If you were being honest, you would admit to yourself that you long much more for the heat of Her cook fire than Her wisdom, but this would be your humanity talking. Forget all that you are now, aside from Her subject, and enter into the Hermit Queen's den.

Easily you find Her there, stoking a fire so hot that She wears only the white pelt of some unknown animal over Her bony shoulders. Her lined face tells you She was expecting you, Her sharp nod affirms you were invited, and Her eyes, black as icy onyx, tell you this may be the conversation of your life. You swallow, but the heat of the flames melts your trepidation.

"Please." She motions for you to sit at Her side. "But take off your coat. You must be roasting!"

You obey, settling down next to Her crystalline throne like a wolf with much loyalty and infinite trust.

"Tell me, child," She begins, holding Her fire poker like a scepter. "Do you know who you truly are in the deepest pit of your soul? In the darkest, shadowy corner of your being?"

You hesitate to say yes, for the journey to Her has taken much from you. The threats to your survival have robbed you of your identity, softened your ego from hardened citrine to runny egg yolk.

"No," you admit. "No, I don't know who I am. Not anymore."

The Hermit Queen erupts into a cackle so loud that a bit of the ceiling crumbles, rolling down the wall in brittle chunks.

She speaks between piercing guffaws. "Not anymore!" Then She collects Herself. "Oh, dear. Well, you're in a pickle, aren't you?" She starts giggling again.

You sigh, unsure of the humor in your identity crisis.

"Young one, such wisdom there is in your words! If you have no idea who you are, then you are truly sager than anyone who claims such certainty."

You frown, and She continues: "A woman who thinks herself all-knowing may rattle off any number of roles she plays, saying I am a mother, a daughter, a doctor, I am this, I am that. My dear, none of those would be true, for she is so much more."

There is a small welling of anger in your blood now, and the heat of the Hermit's fire has made you bold. You did not come all this way, risking your very life, only to be told you are nothing. You shake your head, stand, and speak, no longer the faithful dog at the Queen's side.

"I have come here seeking the wisdom of the North, and you are offering me riddles."

The Queen bubbles in laughter again, and you grow impatient waiting for Her to quiet.

"Ah, my child, you will not like what I'm about to tell you, but I'm going to say it anyway." There is no smile on Her face when She stands, facing you with ferocity in Her ancient eyes. "The wisdom of the North is this: You are whole and perfect in this moment, as you are. Any growth and transformation in this life comes merely from digging up all that lies beneath the snow." She motions to the mouth of the cave. "There! Outside! It is pristine, unmarred, monochromatic, and peaceful, but all that is superficial nonsense, for the marrow of the Earth Mother is beneath all that, and it is muddy, wounded, *real*, and far more interesting."

Her voice becomes a harsh snarl as She continues, and the walls of Her palace begin to rattle. You take a step toward the exit, feeling a chill at your back.

"The wisdom of the North is the wisdom of the Crone who tells you of the meaninglessness of labels and names. You are, right now, all you are meant to be, but you have to get on your knees and dig through the frozen layers with your bare hands."

Large ice boulders begin to fall all around you now, and you run for the way out. She calls after you.

"Your soul is begging for you to shed all that they said you should be. Find yourself beneath the frigid face that you present to the world, the face that protects you from rejection and isolation. Find yourself in the not-knowing. Find yourself in stillness. Find yourself in the spaces between the inhales and exhales."

All that was white goes to black now, and the last memory you have is of the Hermit Queen's final words to you: "There is a part of your deep self, my child, that is absolutely unshakable. Inside this spine-deep core lies the truth: You are everything. It is difficult to articulate your identity when who you truly are is the all-encompassing, eternal death-birth-death dance of the cosmos, and there is a melancholy in that challenge. Herein lies both the grief and the wisdom of the North, with the burden of realizing the authentic, invaluable worth of the self, much like gazing upon a never-ending snowscape."

Know the merit of the North's direction. Know the glittering diamond worth of your being. Much clarity resides in the act of pure, wild, and untainted survival. The North grants women a singular focus: to feed, house, and meet the most basic needs of the deep self. Much comfort resides in the North's endurance; it has always been there, it always will be, and the Witch has a similar everlasting essence in her bones.

YOUR WONDER AND SPIRITUAL INTEGRITY
The Witch's East

The East holds our human quest for spirit-centered integrity. While the North is tangible and heavy, the East is airy, light, and full of subtle spaces in which spirit can live. The call to honor the spirit as an integral aspect of the self, just as profound as our bodies and our minds, is timeworn and treasured. While many would argue this point, I will tell you that religiosity and spirituality are not one and the same. The call to fully and unapologetically embody the wild woman archetype resonates in the East like a sultry siren's voice writhing atop a spring wind; it is a call to claim your spiritual integrity as a Witch and by extension to quench your thirst for this: a deep knowledge of your higher, divine purpose as a woman born into a pivotal time of planetary evolution.

The East is the direction of the newborn's first wail, and we must acknowledge the bewildering, blissful mystery that is birth. Witnessing the moment when a freshly born baby, be it human or otherwise, is welcomed into this world from womb, egg, or other miracle is akin to seeing the very essence of spirit. You, my love, are divine feminine spirit, and the Gods-Goddesses-All-Things-Holy of this world, in every region and throughout time, live in you just as they live in a newly birthed life. Feel the East now at your sacred crown chakra, and inhale the immortal beloved.

A woman's declaration to the East is one of the affirmed sanctity of self. The East feeds her need for universal connection and otherworldliness. She turns to the East when she craves psychic input and intuitive knowing. She turns to this direction of spirit to unlearn all that she has been taught about rigid religiosity. A Witch cries out to the

East to infuse a spiritual enlivening into the circle, lifting the veil ever so slightly, permitting the virtuous and unchanging light of consciousness to enter.

Sensing the Sacred: A Fearless Welcome

Raise your arms and spread your fingers wide as you face East, Sister of the Wild Wind. Let the gust fill your sails and lift you high above the Earth. Close your eyes and surrender to weightlessness and billowed purpose. Let yourself be tossed about like a seed, vowing to bloom wherever the blowing mystery decides to plant you.

Welcome the ethereal spirits of the East as harbingers of the sacred, and listen to their voices fearlessly as they whisper words of both childlike innocence and elder wisdom. Do not be afraid, Kind Witch of the Eastern Sky, for the sun is rising in front of your face. Feel the glow of illuminated spirit casting your features in a new shape, for you are now a winged angel. You are fearlessly and ferociously flying, Witch-Seraphim, and these wings are those you grew long after you leaped into the wind. The East begs you not only to trust in the purpose Spirit has for you but also to surrender to it with all that you are, for you face the direction of miracles. Know the East now for the gifts that it grants. Sense the mystery of not-knowing, and see the merit in active presence and conscious being.

The Angel's Vidya: Feather Seeing with Yogic Gaze

Breaking our spiritual patterns can indeed be painful, but it need not be so arduous all the time. We have much to learn from the weightlessness of spirit and much to gain from the release of judgment. For this yogic practice, you need only a single feather found in nature or purchased from a cruelty-free supplier. Do not hold the feather in your hand but, rather, let this small bit of nature's perfection rest lightly atop your left palm which, in turn, lies in stillness on your left knee. Fix your gaze on the feather now, and let your thinking mind run through all that it knows about this thing; your ego-voice will tell you that it once belonged to a creature, and perhaps it even knows what kind of animal this feather adorned. Such intelligence your thinking mind has, Witch! Your mind may tell you of the patterns and colors decorating this beautiful thing, and it may even try to reason why the feather might be colored or shaped this way. Your mind may rattle through a memory or two in which a feather played a key role. What an amazing life you've had, Wise Mother! Your ego-mind wants to claim ownership over everything you perceive; it has a natural arrogance, so allow this part of you to take over for a time. Let your thinking mind busy itself so much that it yearns to rest.

Permit your mind to run through some of its thoughts, knowing that this may take several minutes or longer, depending on the depth of your caring for and knowledge of feathers. If you keep your gaze affixed on this magick tool used by animals for navigating air and water, my Spirit-Sister, at a certain point a shift will occur. You will no longer view this object as a feather. Suddenly, and often without warning, you will not know what this thing is that you hold in your hand. You will see the feather with pure clarity. Any judgments and patterns you have associated with this thing will dissolve completely, and you will be left with a piece of profound insight: You are this feather, and this feather is you. No distinction exists between you and it.

In this act of clearest sight and sacred gaze, you are gifted with the knowledge of the East. The East shows you that the magick of Spirit exists in all things and only just out of our everyday reach. In order to sense the lightness of our higher selves, we must systematically shed the patterns of our learning. We are conditioned to judge, categorize, and separate, but the Wild Woman of the East knows that such conditioning is the source of much suffering, individual and collective. To gaze upon anything completely unburdened by what we think we know is to experience a particular liberation. The East will set you free, my winged Witch; now fly!

A woman comes to a point in her life when she ceases to associate growth with layering more and more knowledge, skill, and experience atop one another in a looming cake of all flavors. Faced with the pending topple and risk of being forever buried under her own thick icing of patterns, she begins to peel back and cast off assumptions and judgments. At this point in her life, which is not dependent on any particular life stage, the woman begins to see the merit in the Great Unlearning. She starts to dismantle outmoded belief systems and send bits of flaky, superficial, sweetness into the dust. The woman knows the true East when she knows absolutely nothing except the never-ending essence of her own spirit.

YOUR WILDFIRE
The Witch's South

Ponder the qualities of a wildfire, my love, for these are the same traits embodied by the South. The South is a volatile, passionate agent of desire and transformation; it will not be contained, and the belly flame at your solar plexus chakra is drawn to the South and all that this alchemical direction promises. To truly know the South, you must drop your consciousness down deep into your molten core, leaving behind the ethereal Eastern light and diving into the lusty lava that is the boiling blood of the Earth.

The vitality of the South is akin to the hot juices of the wild woman's nature; it gets easily suppressed in our overbuilt world. A woman needs — at the ends of her electric nerves she *needs* — to taste her own unbridled sexuality. We are taught to associate the wild with loss of control, with emotional immaturity, and with irrationality. The dangers of the hysterical woman and risks of being perceived as she-who-will-not-be-tamed are embedded in our collective unconscious and have called us away from the South. A Witch calls out to this sultry direction in order to reclaim the wild as wholly natural, sacredly sexual, and quintessentially her own. This is the direction of the spiritually erotic and soulfully raw.

The Temple Dancer's Awakening

You know the South in your Witch's womb and belly centers; She is at once sultry and willful. The South is the direction that energizes the circle, injecting the space with the potential for authentic fusion. Stand now, coin-belted and bare-breasted Temple Dancer, with your feet rooted hip distance from one another and knees ever so slightly bent. Raise your arms high and form a triangle with your thumbs and forefingers touching, the remaining fingers spread wide like the wings of a phoenix.

Close your eyes and begin to feel a rising in your pelvic bowl that lifts to belly center. Envision this energy as a flaming figure eight connecting your sacral and solar plexus chakras. Let the energy of the South snake up your low spine and awaken your nerve endings. Feel a pulse of electricity at your core, throbbing in time with your belly's beating blood. Now shift your hips to the left without uprooting your feet, and thrust your heart upward. Shine your belly with the light of a thousand candles. Shift your hips forward, and stick out your tongue. Woman, you are the Goddess of Transformation, and this wild world has been waiting for your arrival! Shift your hips right, and know yourself as the embodiment of sweltering sensuality and ecstatic, wanton desire. Shift your hips left and declare yourself the sole owner of your body, now and forever. Dance now as if the global curtains have been raised. Dance as if the world were bowing down to your liberation. Dance as if the sun itself were powering your alchemical body.

To be wild is to feel the pulse of spirit in the body. To be wild is to relish the heat on your lips and to proclaim the holiness of your sex to every church, temple, and mosque. Scrawl your name on the sacred texts, and show them who you are! There is defiance in your wildness only because they have given you rules incompatible with your divinely feminine nature, so, *yes*, reject these notions that would question your sanity and liken the wild woman to one who needs to be caged.

Energizing Desire with Flame: A High-Fire Ritual

You have come to this forest, my Sister, to seek out the fires of transformation. What you did not know was that these fires were seeking you. Look behind you! Face South! Roaring to your left is the Bonfire of Purification and, to your right, the Flames of Manifestation. Scrawled on the paper you hold in your left hand are all the obstacles to your heart's desire; these are both internal, such as fear, self-doubt, and distrust, and external, such as outmoded relationships and lack of resources. In your right hand you hold a heartfelt and poetic description of what you truly, most authentically want; were there no obstacles, this dream would already have come to fruition.

Honor the obstacles as having served their purpose, even if this purpose has been hidden from you. Offer gratitude even to that which seems dark or painful, for we draw much power from our woundings. When you feel ready, toss your list of obstacles into the Bonfire of Purification, and watch it burn. Feel a lightening in your belly, and trust that the fire has purified these barriers to freedom. Do not cling to these heavy burdens simply because they are ingrained in your patterning. You may need to forget what you have learned and melt the ice of stagnation.

Call to mind your desires now, Witch of the Red-Hot Star, and hug the other paper to your heart. Feel what it is to want. Harness that energy not as demeaning or basic but, rather, as integral to your humanity. To change is human, and to activate this transformation from your energetic womb is feminine. Relish the thought of attaining what you want. Know it as having already happened. It is not a fantasy; it is as real as your guts and the ribs that contain them. When you feel ready, cast your desires into the Flames of Manifestation. Feel at your core the fire feeding your dreams, offering its energy to all you hold sacred and true about your future. Reject, in this moment, the notion that time is linear; instead, embrace the knowledge that your desire, at some point in our time-space-spiral of a universe, has happened. Right now, there is a *you* who has attained the life her soul designed for her, and she is bowing deeply in gratitude to the southern fires for all they have gifted her.

The South is a great teacher, my love. Listen to the wisdom of the wild and know yourself as an agent of change. Women who embrace the South act to fuel transformations in their own lives and in the world around them; these women are no victims, and they sit steadfast with tall backs and set jaws as much as they undulate under the full moon. A

Witch calls to the South to affirm the sanctity of her own will and the holiness of both her emotionality and sexuality. A Witch of the South is wild and hot, and she will not be closeted in the cool, dark, and small.

YOUR MYSTERY
The Witch's West

The West is the direction of watery mystery; it is the fertile unknown, and it is all that teems beneath the surface. The West is centered in the waters of the body as well as in the sacral and third-eye chakras. You know the West, Sister, when you swim into the gray-black ocean, holding your breath and diving deeper down, down, and down farther still. You have no idea if or when you will resurface; such is the call of the West. It is where your knowledge and experience end, my love, and the real work begins.

To fear the West is to fear the dark. A woman who loses touch with the West has forgotten the thrill of not-knowing. Her relationship with the spiral of nature is near severed by the loss of the West, for it is a fear-born rejection of the cycle's completion. Kiss the West every day by tasting, just for a moment, the impermanence of all things. Hold the West tenderly against your bare-breasted heart, and let it whisper to you haunting secrets of dark moons and the nights spent floating on open water. A Witch calls to the West to affirm that she does not know everything and to welcome the sweet mystery of the holy dark.

Shape-Shifting under the Mermaid's Moon

The receding wave pulls the sand from under your bare feet, and you dig your toes deeply into the salty wet. Your skirt twists around your knees, and you hold your hands in an inverted triangle at womb-center, thumb touching thumb, forefinger touching forefinger, and the remaining fingers spread wide in front of your pelvis. Face West, away from or toward Mother Ocean, close your eyes, and sink into your depths. Roll in the endless, creative potential that lives inside you, and honor the mermaids' underwater dance of death-birth-death.

For whom, for what, do you long, Witch? Forget all that now, for the West may well have another plan for you, and there is not a damn thing you can do about it. The West is the surrender of the feminine, and it holds all the energies that are, as yet, unseen and unknown: the parts of the cosmos even our most brilliant scientists have yet to fathom and the wealth of power inside the human soul even the most gifted psychic cannot see. The West begs you to shape-shift into the curious mermaid you are, creating and romancing without actively trying to affect the trajectory of your journey.

While the South is active and purposeful, the West is receptive and fluid. Both fire and water hold the magickal properties of purification, but water's cleansing powers are less destructive and heated. The ways of the West are the ways of the water element: fluid, cleansing, subtly powerful, and way-finding. Water can exist as solid, liquid, and vapor; so, too, the essence of woman is heavy body, creatrix mind, and universally connected, ethereal spirit.

Opening to the Death-Life-Death Beauteous Spiral

Lie belly down near any natural body of water, and let your crown face the western mystery. If you cannot be near water, attune to the rushing waters deep underground and proceed as if this were a meditation. Feel the pulse in your belly, and breathe into the grass and dirt. Hear the sounds of a watery world, be it ocean, lake, river, or stream, and consider yourself a masterful work of art. You were painted this way, with all the curved lines and brilliant colors of a mural that makes people weep at its beauty. You were painted in this scene, with the water, sky, and your other surroundings the perfect complement to your body's miraculous shapes. You were painted here as a mystical Undine, and, like all works of art, you are but a temporary physical manifestation of the soul's creative power.

I am asking you now to open to a notion to which most people, out of a flawed attempt to self-preserve, are purposefully closed. Feel the heavy layers of your body's physical form: your hair, your skin, your muscles, your organs, your blood, and your bones. Embrace the impermanence of these parts of you, honoring your soul as so much more ethereal and enduring but, nonetheless, affirming that you, like the life around you in this natural place, will one day meet with death. Trust death as a Great Transformation, no more fearful than birth, and imagine that all that lies on this ground is the white of your bones, painted here by the Mystery.

The West calls you to look into the fanged faces of all that scares you and find the lessons to be learned there. If you were never to leave this scene, if you really were naught more than a pile of bones, what would you have learned from the life you've lived? Why would your soul's path include the wounds and blessings it did? Most important, what lessons would wait for you in the next life, once the spiral of death-life-death began turning for you again? Ponder these questions without clinging to certainty regarding your answers, and you will truly know the West.

Verses of the Holy Feminine
Parable of the Erotic Compass

The prodigal daughter belonged to no one, and yet she yearned to be found and claimed by a great something. She wept in her solitude, her bare back pressing against bark, lusting for sacred relationship with the Holy Wild. Until she discovered her soul-place in the majestic mountains, she was not going back to the good-girl life. She would stay here among the Mother oaks, here among the spotted fawns, here among the mossy stones, and here among the birdsong and mysterious evening sounds.

She turned her gaze North now, opening her legs wide and surrendering to a garnet-red burst of energy low in her sacrum; it made her gasp, and she sprouted tiny roots from her pelvic bones that descended deep and slow into the mud. Her eyes turned to the East, and a cool breeze sent by Aphrodite herself licked the bare places on her body; she reached her right arm long in reverence to her own erotic innocence, and then the South called to her. A sunbeam sent direct from a God-Star and meant only for her ignited the back of her heart, and she arched her spine in ecstasy. Her head rolled to gaze westward over her left shoulder and her lips parted to the watery mystery just as the rain began to fall.

"I am here," she whispered. "I am here. I am here. I am here." She belonged to this place, and it lived in her as much as she lived in it. In this world, she was wholly and freely home.

THE SACRED BOUNDARY
Casting the Circle

Witch of the Four Directions, you have now felt how these sacred energies live inside your feminine soul and perfect body. For now let your hands be your wand and your blade, and hold a fierce confidence at your heart center. Practice opening and closing this sacred boundary by affirming your ecological position in your world. Hone the skill of circle-casting by maintaining a fierce presence of place, and your inner Witch will open her eyes wide.

Stand rooted facing the North, arms at your side like branches and all ten fingers pointed downward. Raise your chin, and feel where the energies of the North meet the essence of this direction inside you, the endurance and sustainability of the Earth Mother meeting your own steadfast ground. Now shout: *Sacred energies of the North, strengthen, embolden, and ground this circle!* Turn to the East now, my love, and feel the wind on your face. Raise your arms high and wide, calling to mind your spiritual wisdom, your sense of innocence, and your Crone-like nature. Call into the night: *Sacred energies of the East, enliven, enlighten, and clarify this circle!* Turn to the fiery South, and form a triangle with your hands, harvesting the belly fire and awakening to your own power. You are everything, Goddess of the Blaze, so raise your voice: *Sacred energies of the South, awaken, energize, and transform this circle!* Turning to the West, move the triangular mudra to your womb, with index fingers pointed to the Earth. Know, without fear, the mystery and magick of the Western direction. Feel the liberation in the void, the peace that rests in the gaps of your experience and knowledge, and the serenity of the watery unknown. Call out: *Sacred energies of the West, drench this circle in magick and mystery!* The circle has been cast now, my Sister, and, as you turn to face the North once more, affirm these words with all the esteem of a lifelong Witch: *This circle is closed.*

Sit inside your sacred boundary now, my love, and sense what surrounds you there. You are protected and whole, nourished and shielded by the natural energies of this world. Your magickal work is amplified in this space, and the echoes of ancient voices resonate in your ears here. Know who you are in this circle, worthy Witch, for you have earned your place here. When you feel ready, stand and turn to the West, framing your womb and calling out these words: *Sacred energies of the West, thank you. Go in peace.* Turning to the South with triangle mudra raised high, offer this chant: *Sacred energies of the South, thank you. Go in peace.* Turn to the East, arms still raised but outstretched and offer your farewell before turning North. Point your arms downward and bid a grateful good-bye to the direction of pure ground.

YOUR PLACE IN THE WILD WORLD

The circle is open now, Mistress of Manifestation, and you have felt the energetic shift inside and around you. You felt the high-frequency vibration of a circle closed, and you trusted in your ability to honor and call the directions. Know spellwork as a shaping and directing of these same energetic forces, much as an artist wields materials to birth something new. Know your own body as a buzzing hive of tiny magickal circles housing the nutrients of Earth, the space of the East, the pranic life-force of the South, and the fertile fluids of the West. With this understanding, my Sister, you will begin to remember how spells are cast. Rest assured, all will seem familiar, for you certainly are a Woman Most Wild.

Chapter 6

A Priestess-Healer's Spellwork

Spirit-born and skillful spellcrafting is an art no less beauteous than a fluid ballet or a fine-lined sculpture. Your medium is the many-energied universe, your palette the sacred circle, and your studio the sacred temple of the natural world. You will seek and hone your own style of spellwork, discerning Sister, and you will work to honor your unique perception of the greatest good. I have affirmed your complete autonomy as a Witch, my love, and I stand fierce behind this proclamation: Your spiritual agency is perfect. In rebinding the Witch to the healer archetype, integrating the yogic practice of *ahimsa*, or nonharming, into your spellwork becomes a complex endeavor. Many Witches reject the nonharming premise as overly limiting, and I am not one to pass judgment on the spiritual freedom of any woman. However, I do believe that your spellwork reflects an intimate conversation with the Mystery and, moreover, your hope for a peaceful and empathic world.

Harm is subjective, and I believe it is the practitioner's task to ascertain the roles of harm and compassion in every spell cast. In *The Global Heart Awakens*, Anodea Judith writes, "When we feel with another, we open to compassion, which literally means to be with another's passion." In permitting compassion — for yourself, your inner circle, and the whole of the world — to undergird your spellwork, you affirm that these are the qualities you want to see embodied by the human community. Every spell you cast will be all the more powerful for its embodiment of this nonharming ethic, the very essence of the sustainable feminine. Your spells of healing, manifestation, and protection are all guided by a beacon of divine and ultimate love for the wildness and interconnectivity of all things. If you resonate with the wild healer archetype, you hold a sacred responsibility to support positive global transformation, to work for the healing of the Earth Mother, and to engage in a fierce practice of self-care.

Certain herbs will call your name so loudly you can hear them, and any number of stones, rhymes, and energy-raising techniques will do the same. I recommend, with all the love I have for you, that you begin creating simple spells that are birthed from your own Witch's consciousness as much as mimicked from another practitioner's Book of Shadows. Consider a new painter, aware of her inborn talent but uneducated in design or color theory; is it better for her to attempt to copy a masterpiece or to experiment with her own unique ways of creating? You will find your own Craft by letting your soul-voice guide you. Surrender your fears of doing it wrong, and cast your circle strong.

A woman is called to make magick as she is called to create; this call is inborn. We are taught to suppress our yearning for magick during and after adolescence, and a woman learns that the mystical is the stuff of fantasy, to associate the Witch with the fairy-tale antagonist, and to never dare assert her Craft, should she come to know it, openly and visibly. Your Witch's hands are wise, my love. You are able to shape the energies of this world, to let them bend to your will, and to infuse with your own power the outcomes you most desire. The appropriation of a woman's magick, often by framing it as both evil and nonexistent, is another act of her spiritual oppression. Do not let your ability be invalidated, my love, but do not take it for granted, either. Spellcraft and meaningful ritual design demand at least intermittent practice. Slowly weave magick into your world like any other newly found but dearly loved craft; do not become feverishly obsessed. Begin slowly, but be certain to begin.

The Three Gateways of Ethical Magick

Consider ethical magick untainted by ego-born power and dominance. When your magick is ethical, it is not only a stronger force but also an agent of positive social changes. Let your magick reflect the same qualities you want to see in the human community. Let every spell be a conversation with the universe during which you say, as clearly as you can, what kind of world you want to live in. Your spell is a reflection of your truth, just as an artist's masterpiece is her or his reflection of a great and fierce authenticity, as channeled through artistic vision. Ask yourself if your spell would pass through the Three Gateways of Ethical Magick; this initial assessment will become second nature as your work as a Witch evolves.

The Gate of Service and Truth will let nothing pass that is not positively transformative for the subject of the spell. In yoga this gate is the ethical boundary of *ahimsa*, nonharming, and it is the most critical consideration in any spell. If you are casting a prosperity spell, for instance, will the intended outcome truly serve you? Are you being honest with yourself about how this outcome would affect you and those around you? Ask yourself: Does it serve? Is it true? Is it working for your perception of the greater good? If so, your intent is pure, and you may move confidently to the second gate.

The Gate of Desire will let nothing pass that is not fueled by passion or yogic *tapas*. If you do not truly care about the spell you are crafting, then it will be akin to a boat with a gaping hole at its bottom. While there are many ways to raise energy, ultimately it is your desire, as the feminine divine embodied, that will fan the magickal flame. The holy power of a woman's desire cannot be discounted, for it is truly a force to be reckoned with. Ask yourself: Do you want this? Does it speak to your soul's truth? Does it resonate with or bolster your frequency? If so, emboldened Witch, proceed to the final gate.

Last, but very important, the Gate of Surrender will not allow a spell to pass that you are not ready to release. Regardless of how attached you are to the intention, you must be ready to let the spell go once it is performed. You craft the spell, perform the spell, then surrender the magick to the Mystery. The act of surrender permits the necessary universal energies to rise to your aid. Before you surrender the spell, your magick is limited by your perceptions and expectations; when you release it, however, the possibilities of its fulfillment are infinite. In yogic ethics, this gate is *isvara pranidhana*, or laying your work at the feet of God-Goddess-Mystery. Are you ready to release this spell once it is done? Can you truly own your desire for the spell's intention to come to pass without clinging to its exact outcome? Remember, my love, the universe is not framed by our linear, masculine time; it is circular, and commanding your spell to come to fruition by a certain date rarely works. Witch of the Spiral Moon, open yourself to your power without attaching yourself to or defining yourself by it, and the Mystery will rise to support you with miracles as countless as the stars. Passing through the third gate, you affirm that your Craft is truly worthy of divine attention, and you are ready to remember your She-Magick.

HEALING THE SHE-MAGICK WAY

Healing spells support greater holistic authenticity and growth for body, mind, and spirit; they may be directed toward any number of places, including but not limited to the spell's crafter, individuals who have given permission to be the spell's subject, past-life woundings, the holy planet, or parts of the global community. Honor the vibrancy of the sacred self in every healing spell you craft; honor the ways in which the illness, wound, or deficiency has served you or the spell's subject; and, very important, honor the ways in which the elements resonate in the healing process. As a Witch of the Wild World, you are responsible for working your healing magick for yourself and others, honoring the sustainability of the human community of Gaia's children. Women are uniquely positioned not only to bandage but also to truly heal the bleeding wounds of our world; indeed, much of our society's pitfalls have stemmed from the intentional, strategic, and long-standing suppression of women's power. In taking back the magick that is rightfully yours, you are already acting as global healer.

Whole-Heart Healing for the Earth

Human beings have an intimate connection with the Earth's electromagnetic field; it affects us, and we affect it. The full moon has called you to cast your circle tonight in the name of healing the Earth Mother's heart. Gather your tools, my love! Run into the night with your basket full and your heart open, or go to your wild sanctuary in your home. Ideally, carry a carnelian stone and rosemary, along with a good deal of raw compassion. You may substitute any symbols of manifestation and Mother Nature if you are unable to acquire those recommended resources. Find a place where you know She can see you, then gather stones to set in the four directions.

Shield your aura, as directed in chapter 1, and know that nothing can pass through your crystalline armor. Now cast your circle just as firmly, moving in the directions from North to West, shaping your body according to the elemental correspondences. The circle is closed, and all is coming! Can you hear your own heart-drum mirroring the pulse of the Earth? Place the carnelian stone before you so it touches the ground. Sink into a deep mantra now, repeating aloud the sacred being states of love, gratitude, and empathy: *Love, gratitude, empathy. Love, gratitude, empathy.* Become a channel for these pure functions of a healthy heart, and plant your hands on the ground. Close your eyes and envision the heart of the Earth. What colors are there? How is the energy moving? How big does it feel? Are there places in the Earth-Heart that seem muddy or weak-energied? Send your healing light there, down through your Witch's hands into the subterranean core of Gaia.

When you feel ready, let your eyes open and begin to plant your carnelian, a stone Earth designed for heart health, deep into the fertile ground, be it out in nature or within a pot of sacred soil. If you feel called to do so, offer some words as the spell draws to a close; these might be words of immense compassion or soulful thankfulness toward the Earth for supporting you and those you love most truly. Sprinkle the rosemary atop the planted stone, and seal your work. You may sit in this closed circle for as long as you have, but, when ready, open the circle as recommended in chapter 5, moving counterclockwise from West to North. Inside this space now is a layer of fierce love energy and nourishing power. Once you call out that the circle is open, release this energy deep into the Earth, pressing your hands along the electric edge of the energy bubble and pushing it down into the holy ground. Your work is done, Worldly Witch. All blessings be!

The archetype of the wild healer lives within all women, but she has been sequestered in the psychic shadows for so long that bringing her into the light of day may feel like a waste of precious energy and time. The two loudest voices of the ego are the one that wants to keep you small and, quite conversely, the one that wants you to be in complete control. The wild healer is neither weak nor all-powerful; she is driven by the heart and concerned with empathic connection. Harvest your inner wild healer when crafting the spells to soothe burning wounds and aching wrongs; she is there, and she has been waiting for you.

Salve for the Mother Wound

We women have suffered the loss of the powerful feminine divine. With deity presented to us solely in its male form, we stand as orphaned sisters who share the same wound. Very often this wound manifests in the unconscious placement of lofty expectations on our own human mothers; we are looking to them to fill a great void, a void they too feel as women, and a void that can only be filled with a thorough embrace of the divine feminine on a social level; this is not to say that there are not mothers in this world who have allowed their own shadows to fester and rot, manifesting in severe and often brutal harm to their children. In this moment, consider that every mother, given the lessons she has learned, the sacrifices she has made, the patterns she lives out, and the

Mystery's design, has done the best she could for her children with the internal and external resources she had available.

Salve for our mother wound, Sister, can be brewed with magickal ingredients, for the work of sacred spellcraft is the work of awakening Her. Every time we reclaim the name of Witch, we feel a stirring in our bones and beneath our bare feet; this is the divine feminine's invigoration, the change we have been awaiting for millennia. Your part in this global transformation is significant, Wild One, so do not diminish the power of mother-wound healing. Build your altar and cast your circle strong now, for we have much work to do together.

In addition to a white candle, dried mugwort, and white sage, gather reflections of your matrilineal line: pictures and symbols of your daughters, your sisters, your mother, and your grandmothers. Objects will suffice if actual photographs are not available, and make sure, my divine Sister, that you yourself are represented as well. Organize these items linearly, with your daughters and granddaughters represented to the right of your picture and all those wise elders who came before you to the left. Know this soul-inspired arrangement as your matrilineal design. Know that in healing your own wound, you heal the wounds of all women in and even beyond your line.

Inside your closed circle, stand before your Mother Altar. Light the white candle and prepare the mugwort and sage in a burning bowl. Close your eyes and hold your hands above your own picture, palms facing the altar. Drop your consciousness down deeply into your womb, and then give permission to your mother wound to show itself to you as a dark river of thick water. Underlying resentment, unprocessed emotions, troublesome memories, and a wide spectrum of deeply seated pain pervades the subterranean waters of our mother wound. Imagine you stand ankle-deep in this body of warm, flowing, thick, womb-water, and you can feel the energies of your children's children as well as your great-great-grandmothers in the rushing current. Now imagine crouching down and allowing your hands to drop deep into the waters before you; as your magick hands drop down, down, and down farther still, the water around them thins and grows clearer. As you move your hands in this vision, so, too, do you move your hands over the altar, clearing the wounded waters in your mind's eye and concurrently healing the wounds of your matrilineal line.

Feel a pulsing in your sacral center as you do this, and allow any visions or emotions that surface to come. Suppress nothing, Brave-heart, for the Crones of your bloodline are bowing deeply in your favor now. They stand around you in solidarity. Can you feel them? The ghosts of your grandmothers are honoring your bravery and holding their fists high as the river around you clears and runs with a vibrant light. What color is your river becoming? How swiftly do the waters move? Stay until the work feels done, and then let your eyes open. Face your line like the healing warrior you are, and light the sage and your mugwort. Now, moving from left to right, compassionately and wholeheartedly smudge every symbolic representation of every woman in your line. Affirm this for each and every member of your feminine lineage: *Woman, I bow to you. Your wounds are my wounds, and my healing is your healing.*

When you feel ready, open the circle, but allow the candle to burn safely down on its own. If you feel called to do so, you may write a letter of closure or forgiveness to your mother and burn it with the ashes in your burning bowl. Gift the ashes to your Mother Tree, and honor the profound blessings you have been given as a woman in *this* time and *this* place. Blessed be our grandmothers. Blessed be our mothers. Blessed be Woman.

Healing is not a layering-over or a sewing-up of the past; it is an eternal practice of awareness through which you consciously acknowledge the relationship between what *is* and what must be. A true healer promises nothing. She digs deep, calls forth, and busts open. There is no inevitable closure, but there is always a felt change. You are a healing alchemist, Wild One, and we are born of the same earthly womb.

MANIFESTING THE SHE-MAGICK WAY

The magick of manifestation exists in an intricate web of universal energies and unseen connections; it is far more complex than the mere, albeit passionate, desire for a particular outcome. To truly manifest your dreams, they must be part of the future your soul handcrafted for you, they must resonate in your cells as thoroughly and wholly *yours* even before they come to pass, and, most important, you must know in your Witch's bones that this future can be realized. Every cell in your body must believe, with all that it is, that you are truly worthy and deserving of this miracle. You must be willing to do the nonmagickal work necessary to birth your desires, and then, with seeming contradiction, you must be willing to release attachment to the spell's outcome to the universe.

Remembering the Yet-to-Come: Magickal Vision Writing

My Sister, I hold that everything you truly value already belongs to you. In the vastness of the cosmos, a version of you is already enjoying the full realization of all that your soul has dreamed for you. Drop your consciousness to your third eye, and gaze through the diamond-light window there between your brows. Can you see this woman? Write down everything about her, this beauty of strongly held convictions and fully born dreams. Do not write *I*; write *she*. What is *she* doing in this vision? Is she alone? How does she feel? Consider this scene now with all your senses; what does this version of you see, taste, touch, smell, and hear? As you write, if any voices come up that are concerned with practical obstacles, strategy, or how-tos, silence them for now, my love, for they will get their chance to speak.

This magickal vision is your soul's communication of what is most authentically yours. When you hold this vision in your mind's eye you should feel a pulsing at your heart center that is the rhythm of deep, hopeful knowing. As you read over what you have written, your whole body should affirm that this future is yours. Hold your writing at heart center now, and let it resonate with your physical and subtle bodies. Affirm aloud that this dream is *yours*, and then cast your circle around your burning bowl. Now read your vision aloud as if you were reading the most sacred text, for you are. Your voice should reflect the reverence with which you desire this life for yourself as well as the firm knowledge that the universal energies of support will groundswell beneath you to fuel this future. Once finished, set this vision aflame; as it burns, call to mind the vision of yourself once this outcome has been realized; send her all the love and gratitude you have, for she has earned every gift she has been given.

Open your circle when ready, Blessed Sister, and surrender to the magick. Look for nods from the divine in the coming hours and days, for you will receive signs that all is coming; do not ignore these opportunities, no matter how seemingly coincidental, for the Mystery is watching you. Prove that you are listening to It as much as It is listening to you, and you will be dazzled by the countless miracles sent your way.

Live your life by setting your feet firmly on solid ground, creatively and sensually exploring your world in order to break patterns and burning down everything that does not belong, and then manifest your vision in the space you have opened with the gifts you are given. Such is the path of the Yogini-Witch, and such is the path of the Woman Most Wild. So mote it be.

Calling In Abundance and Grace: Gifting Global Prosperity

Manifestation magick born of fear is weak, but that born of love is a formidable force, indeed. Be wary of using your magick solely for personal gain, empathic Sister, for you were born precisely at this time for a reason. Wield your magick for the good of yourself as well as for the good of *all*, and you will be afforded true and endless abundance. You have considered what you want for yourself; now consider your vision for our global community. Were you the Mistress of the Universe, able to easily shape the social landscapes of our future like so much clay, what would you want for our divine world? Be specific, and write out your hope for your children's children.

Now consider what values underlie this global vision of yours; perhaps equality and sustainability? Perhaps abundance and freedom? These are values you hold very deeply in your Witch's soul, and they are your truest currency. Now, my love, center your consciousness at your root chakra, low at the base of your spine, and ask yourself how prolific these values are in your life. For instance, if you highly value the freedom of personal choice, and truly want everyone in the world to have an abundance of the same freedom, ask yourself how much freedom you have in your own life. Now, my love, ask what part of the global vision you need more of in your life. What do you value deeply for the whole world yet have little of for yourself?

You need no materials, but cast your circle strongly, with you at its center. Coming to a seated position, engage *mulabandha*, your body's root-support system, by lifting your pelvic floor, and then place your hands at your sides on ground. Now, lift your heart up ever so slightly, coming into a small backbend if you are able. With your body in this shape, your root is supported and your heart is open. Closing your eyes, imagine that authentic currency, whatever it is, flowing toward you and through you. Know yourself as being energetically gifted with all that you want for the world, filling your Witch's pockets with the priceless riches of boundless abundance. Breathe with this vision now, abundance flowing into heart center on the inhale, being pulled down to your root along the right side of your spine, then, as you exhale, gift this same abundance to the global community, pulling it up from your root to your heart along your left side, breathing the gift of your breath out into the world.

Every breath now becomes a body prayer to abundance, with the most valuable *good* flowing into you and into the cosmic net of our human community on every inhale and exhale. Stay with this for as long as you have before opening the circle, sending the collected energy down deeply in the ground below you by pressing palms to Earth. Your Witch's soul is a cell of the global body of the Earth, which itself is a cell inside this great mystery-riddled universe of ours. Fiercely gifting to yourself what you desire strongly for the world at large is an act of true magick, so, worthy Witch, open your heart and receive all that is coming to you. Open yourself to the possibility that our world holds precisely enough for every innocent child, nurturing adult, and wise elder.

The whole of our economy is based on the nonfeminine principle of scarcity, and this counters what we know in our hearts and wombs to be true. We are socialized to be good capitalistic consumers who spend and hoard our resources largely in response to an indoctrinated fear of not having enough. Women instinctively acknowledge the wild as a context for sufficiency and abundance. No living thing voraciously consumes until it bursts, because the wild feminine is a natural peace-keeper and balance creator. Use your manifestation magick to facilitate sufficiency for all and to converse with the cosmos about how you want the world to be. We live in an abundant world, and there are enough resources to sustain us all, were they allocated with feminine integrity. Orchestrate the new paradigm with every circle you cast, my love, and you play your part in the emerging story of holistic global connection.

PROTECTING THE SHE-MAGICK WAY

While the feminine is undoubtedly concerned with relationship and heart-to-heart connection, it is also true that boundaries in the life of the Witch are sacred and necessary. Though a Witch may be no more vulnerable to a psychic, emotional, verbal, physical, or other form of wall breaching than anyone who is not in tune with their magick, she is positioned to protect herself well. Moreover, my love, the Witch has a responsibility to fortify strong boundaries in order to shield her sacred work safely and consistently. Call to mind the Three Gateways, and remember that your magick must do no harm, whatever you conceive that harm to be. Ethical protection spells shield yourself, your inner circle, the community, a specific population, or other subject from being harmed; they do not offensively attack a particular person. Mind you, plenty of Witches practice hexing in the name of their perception of the greater good; for them, this is true. For me, keeping my magick heart centered rather than born of ego or emotional reaction feels right, but it may not be so for others or for you. Work your protection magick safely and with goodwill, my Sister, and the divine Mystery will guard the boundaries you set with many-armed angels.

Sacred Home Protection: Fortress Keeping for the Wild Woman

A woman's home is her greatest source of root nourishment; it is her sacred temple. Gather these materials, Great Protectress: garlic, sea salt, sage, a white candle, a bell, and a clear quartz crystal for every room in your home. Now, my love, I know this is easier said than done, but declutter your space as much as possible, and open all closets and cabinets. Beginning at the top of your house, in your attic, if you have one, open a window, and light the white candle at the room's center; leave the candle safely burning at the center of the room and light the sage. Holding the sage in your hands, begin to circle out counterclockwise from the candle, moving in slow spirals from the center of the room outward toward the walls. Envision yourself pushing out any stagnant or negative energy as you move, your body becoming a psychic broom. When you come to a closet or cabinet, ring the bell in the corners to break up the collected energy there, then puff some sage into the area. Sprinkle a pinch of sea salt and garlic on all windowsills and doorways, then return to the white candle at the room's center. Now, a second time, spiral out from the room's center but move clockwise this time, envisioning yourself bringing love and light into the space with your very being.

Once the room has been cleared and protected, leave a clear quartz in a part of the room where it will not be disturbed for a few weeks. Go through this process in every room in your home, moving from high to low, and be sure to put extra garlic and sea salt at the main door to your home. Positioning a broom, even if it is a small, symbolic broom, near the door of your home will ward off ill energy, and the universe will respond to your efforts of protection. Watchful Witch, know your own energy and that of your home as existing in an ideal, symbiotic relationship. Keep the energy of your home clear and resonant with your own soul frequency, and your home will do the same for you. Allow your home space to reset you from the energetic exchanges of the day when you return, and know it as a haven for your Witch's work. Honor your home for the magickal space that it is, clearing and protecting it on the solstices and equinoxes, and affirm yourself as both Lady and Guardian of your castle.

Look to your home as a microcosm of your dreamworld. Live in your space as you hope everyone will live, surrounded by bright beauty and handmade goodness. A woman's home is where she finds both quiet solitude and sensual connection. Just as your magick reflects your most deeply held values, so too does your home embody the energy you raise with every spell. Your home, despite its hard edges and many corners, is akin to your sacred circle, so protect it with all that you are.

Shielding the Feminine Collective: Protection Magick for Women of the World

As far as we have progressed in the developed world, my liberated Sister, we still have far longer to go before we reach any genuine level of gender equality. In many parts of our world women are still afforded scant opportunities compared to men, are used as targets for war, and are even still burned for being witches. Work your magick for the feminine collective now, dear one, and I will work it with you, for we are in this together.

Do not take your power and position for granted, my love, and do what you can. Do not feel too helpless, too distant, or too busy. Take the time now, wherever you are, and cast your circle; you need nothing inside the sacred shape aside from your own body and will. Stand firm on your own two feet at circle center, and flip your left palm skyward and right palm down toward Gaia's green ground. Close your eyes, and imagine that you are part of a great circle of women, alive, dead, and yet to be born, who stand with you. Imagine their bodies in the same shape as yours, and know their intent as a perfect mirror to your own; you are protecting the women of our world who cannot protect themselves, and you are rising against injustice with all the magick you have.

Swelling at your solar plexus is the belly flame of will, esteem, and identity, and it is raging with anger at the harm done to women and children around the world. Lift your left arm high now, and imagine you hold a great, flaming sword, and the women with you do the same. Call to mind now the collective feminine wounding done by long-standing and institutionalized societal oppression; if this terrible injustice had a color and shape, what would they be? Imagine it is before you now, and, Witch of the Wounded World, strike at this obstacle with all that you are. Strike a fierce and fatal blow to this enemy before you, and watch it disintegrate into so much ash and smoke.

Repeat this mantra now, Woman Warrior of the Tribe of Transformation: *I protect the women of this world by the power of earth, water, fire, air, and ether. Let no harm come to them or their children. Our daughters are protected, So mote it be. Our mothers are protected. So mote it be. Our grandmothers are protected. So mote it be. So mote it be. So mote it be. By all the magick I have, so mote it be.*

Wild woman spirituality's roots run thick and deep, sunk into the soft loam of our wounded world. The Witch who resonates with the wild healer archetype seeks true justice and balance for all living creatures in our great collective, and she uses her magick accordingly. The wild woman is neither antiman nor antimasculine; she is seeking equality by raising up those who have been victims of oppression historically and continue to feel the effects of institutionalized prejudice. Protect the women of this world, Witch, and you will have done the magick this world needs most right now.

Verses of the Holy Feminine
Redemption Prayer for the Wild Healer

Dearly beloved, we are gathered here today to redeem the Wild Healer, the one who wielded so much feminine fortitude in her holy hands that she was feared, shunned, and cast out. We bow down to her now, this

woman who was much like you, much like me. We have dug up her bones and laid them on our altars. We have lit candles for her, and now we pray that her ghost stand with us when we work our own healing magick for our wounded world.

Stand with us, Wild Healer, when our bodies are shamed, our sexuality caged, and our work discounted as less than. Stand with us when we are too tired to stand up for ourselves, and stand with us when we raise our swords high for the women of this world who yearn for liberation. Stand with us against all oppression, past, present, and future. Stand with us and raise your voice in a war cry against injustice. Stand with us in the most righteously raging solidarity there is, and, whatever you do, do not sit down.

Wild Healer, you are redeemed, for your bones symbolize our birthright. We weep for you, a woman who made vows to the sacred Earth with every seed she planted and every berry she harvested. We weep for the loss of your medicine, and we hold your ethereal hands now as we work our own magick. Wild Healer, you are we, and we are you. In Her name, I pray, amen.

The Rhythms of Magick

Your wild ritual and holy magick are entirely your own. A wealth of correspondences exists for the ideal time, day, and season to work your Craft, but such considerations can be overwhelming as you begin honing your practice. As a very general rule, my Sister, healing and protection spells should be worked as the moon is waxing or full, while protection or banishing spells can be worked as the moon is full or waning. Do not become bogged down by complex when-to rules, for you will find your own way, and you will create your own spell palette colored by your unique experience. Be wary of rules so prolific that you become immobilized in your Craft, and trust that the most righteous Book of Shadows is the one you have written with your own hand. The rhythms of magick live in you as much as outside in the natural world, and this truth, my love, is precisely what makes you a Woman Most Wild.

Chapter 7

The Wild Goddess Ministry

*T*hus far, beloved and newfound Sister, I have affirmed your divinity and invited you to frame the Witch as a wild woman who, while intensely driven by soul and spirit, may claim no religious affinity. I have offered you Witchcraft as a way of being in this world rather than as rule-rigid religion, and I have spoken very little about any particular Goddess, God, or deity. Just as I have charged you to fashion your own magickal repertoire, I also ask you to respectfully explore the Goddesses first as high-energy archetypes before practicing any specific ritual in their reverence. This, my Sister, ensures that you will not unknowingly step into one of the common pitfalls of the beginner practitioner and *use* the Goddesses as culturally appropriated tools rather than establishing a reverent and holy relationship with them.

In this chapter I offer you flexible and introductory practices for understanding your own divinely feminine nature. For a wild woman, internalizing the Goddess is paramount, for she has an intuitive under-standing that divinity is not external to her. When you begin to explore deities as archetypes, you also assess how these holy beings resonate within you. There will be Goddesses to whom you are strongly drawn, and you will begin to feel a close kinship with them because of how their energy resides in your deep Witch's consciousness. I have told you before that you *are* the very essence of the God-Goddess-Mystery, and I meant it. Just as not every vision of an abundant life is the same, not every Witch is drawn to the same manifestations of the divine mas-culine, feminine, and pan-gender deities. It will save you much time and energy, dear one, if you hold steadfast to these three truths: First, not every Goddess and God will speak to your wild soul, and this is as it should be. Second, and more salient, the sacred masculine and feminine deities who do resonate with you will cry out for you to honor them as integral to, not isolated from, your very being. Finally, believing in deity is not at all essential to the way of the Witch. You are no less a Witch if you find no kinship with any Goddess or God, and all choices affecting your spiritual liberation are yours and yours alone.

As mentioned earlier, a common deeply dug hole that many women who have recently harvested their inner Witch step into is the assumption that deities are something to be *used*. A Goddess is not a wand or other magickal tool; She is the Holy Creatrix deserving of de-votion and honor. Be wary of language that urges you to "use" a partic-ular deity for a particular spell, for this is an intention much flawed and ill crafted. Also be sensitive to the dangers of cultural appropriation, knowing that your embodiment of the wild healer archetype is inextri-cably bound to your rejection of oppression. Witches are not cultural imperialists, and the Western woman must work her magick against oppression; very often, this means closely examining why you resonate with a certain deity who is not integral to the culture in which you were raised. Explore and examine with much respectful curiosity and a wholehearted seeker's mentality. Dig deep, and question any practice involving a deity that seems superficial. Asking such questions ensures that you act against a sense of entitlement to any and all cultures and remain respectful of the global community's blessed diversity.

Consider the Goddesses and Gods vibrating around us in the same cosmic web as all subtle energies, albeit at a much higher frequency, and know these sacred Ones as powerful embodiments of your own divinity. As a woman, you are infused with Goddess energy, and every time you acknowledge your divinity, you contribute to the divine feminine vibrations in the universe.

A woman who has been too long separated from the Goddess must dust the soil off her long-buried divinity. She often has to examine beliefs about the Goddess as being fluffy and inconsequential; she learns that these associations were orchestrated by patriarchal traditions, even those of a pagan nature, to render the divine feminine inferior to the divine masculine. Goddesses are as diverse and changeable as the natural world, Woman, and so are you. There is nothing passively pink and too soft about the Goddess, my love, for She is the many-faced power of the feminine. Exploring your Goddess nature should be a practice that moves cyclically, not one that is aggressively and singularly pursued but, rather, slowly integrated into your life and practice as a wild woman during times of both spiritual thirst and abundance.

Exploring Your Goddess Nature

Highest Priestess, you must consider yourself a Goddess in your own right. Divinity is not distant or judgmental; it is inside you as much as it is external to you, and the Goddess-God vibrations that call to you will be those meant for you at this particular point in your life. As you begin your exploration of your Goddess nature, be open to what comes, and trust the Mystery. Surrender to your Goddess nature by believing in something you were told to reject. Woman, you are holy fire, and you hold as much diamond-light electricity inside your soul as any manifestation of God-Goddess-Mystery. You are She who is and will always be, and I lie in whole-body prostration to your awesome power.

Surrendering to She Who Is and Will Always Be: A Waking Meditation

Build yourself a throne of pillows, blankets, and bolsters, Mother of All. Let it be a throne worthy of the task at hand; you are awakening to your own divinity with purpose and passion, and you are affirming yourself as a wise, intuitive, compassionate, empowered, sensual, and abundant creatrix. The raw feminine force that surges and spirals within your blood awaits your direction, and your Witch's soul will be your guide as you clearly see and then affirm your Goddess nature.

Sink into whatever shape your holy body wants to be in, ensuring that your third eye is gazing skyward. You may be seated, in a supported backbend, or lying on the ground. If it is comfortable, you may, Yogic Sister, come into the open-heart-Goddess position; in this shape, your back is supported with a high stack of pillows or rolled blankets so that both your spine and head are cushioned. Your knees fall open wide, with the bottoms of your feet touching. In this shape of reception, surrender to the present moment by tuning into your wild breath. Let the breath fill the belly on the inhale, and feel a soft whisper in the back of your throat on the exhale. Stay with this long enough to anchor your being *here* and *now*.

Drop your thinking mind down to your heart center, and see the subtle energies that vibrate there. Call to mind the frequencies of love and compassion, and give permission for your Goddess-Light to show itself to you. At first you may see only a pinpoint of light, and it may seem to be of a strange color. Affirm aloud *I see you*, and the Goddess-Light will begin to swell and transform. Notice the intense vibrations of your divine light, and then begin to feel its sacred infusion in every cell in your body. Your Goddess-Light sparks inside your bones, your blood, and your organs. Your heart consciousness can see this light nourishing and healing the vital parts of your physical body, igniting your pranic state of aliveness with pure spirit.

Your live-wire being is so awake now! You feel lighter, raw, and magickal, as if your blessed angel's wings have spread wide for the first time in a waking state. See yourself now with a halo of pale light, crowning you like the holy creature you are. You may also see yourself in divine adornments, holding sacred objects, or painted with ancient symbols of feminine fortitude, death, and birth. Take notice of your God-self, and know this divinity as your own, internalized in your very being but no less worthy of worship.

Bringing your attention back to the breath now, let your inhales and exhales be a body prayer to your own sacred soul. Know yourself as having been gifted the cosmic crown of sublime awareness. Now, hallowed Witch, begin to feel the weight of your beauteous body on your soft throne, and bring some small movements into your hands and feet. Let your breath be loud, for it is the breath of the Goddess as she breathes the whole of our cosmic universe into being, and, when you are ready to rise, you will walk in the world with a deep sense of consecrated self-knowledge. Woman, you are a She-God, and you have always been so. Do not discount the worthiness of your will or the weight of your words, for we have been waiting for you.

Divine and majestic being, I have prepared an altar for your awakening, and I commemorate this moment with a prayer of immense gratitude. Thank you for letting me walk this path with you, and thank you for honoring the divine feminine in all women by acknowledging its presence in you. All blessings be, Winged One. All blessings be.

Know that you need not name Her at first. She is She who is. Women coming to know the Goddess are coming to know themselves *as* Goddess, and this demands quite a bit of commitment and, often, a massive infusion of self-esteem. Your spirit light burns so brightly in your belly, slowly but surely melting away the wounds left by others on your self-worth. Their words have not shaped who you are, for She breathed you into being long before you were born.

The Goddess Deck: Personal Prayer Cards for the Wild Woman

In awakening to your Goddess nature, you have likely been called to begin exploring the Goddess-God archetypes that have served our human community for countless generations. You may have seen artfully designed card decks illustrated with the many faces of the Goddess, some of which will call your name loudly, asking to be part of the library you are growing as an eternal student of Mystery. In the spirit of your divine liberation, gather materials to create your own seven-card Goddess deck: blank index cards of a thick weight, drawing materials, scissors, and perhaps magazines and a clear medium for collage.

For one week, beginning on whatever day you choose, personify the Goddess archetype you feel is most needed in your life right now. For instance, if you are vibrating in a state of scarcity, the Goddess to whom you are drawn may be a long-haired, fruit-bearing, gold-crowned Goddess of abundance. If you are being pulled toward romance, your Goddess might be a full-bodied sultry Maiden. If you are in need of guidance or an intuition boost, your Goddess may be a hooded Crone with three eyes. The possibilities are endless, but remember to be true to what you need. Consider your daily Goddess creation to be a reflection of your soul path on that day, and know the Goddess who emerges from your creative consciousness to be no less real than any deity you could research by name.

In creating your cards, you will depict the Goddess in whatever way seems right. Perhaps you will name Her, or perhaps it will seem too soon to call Her anything but Goddess. Know that She has presented Herself to you exactly as She intended, and know that She is there to support you. In creating the cards, you are infusing much magickal energy into the work of spiritual devotion; She knows it. Do not discount your work, no matter how unbeauteous it may seem to you, for She appreciates your efforts. Keep your deck on your altar or somewhere safe, and keep adding to it as you see fit. This work will affirm the divinity inside you as well as cultivate an evolving relationship between you and the sacred feminine.

Remember that there is no one way to be a Witch, and there is no singular path to Goddess study. You may find that you are called to fiercely explore a particular Goddess one moment, and then have your attentions drift toward another holy being the next. She knows you are not forsaking Her. Understand the Goddess energy as dynamic and fluid; it will reach momentous peaks within your psyche and soul just as it will ebb into deep valleys. Be open to fruition and fallows, for such is the way of our nature.

GODDESSES OF THE WORLD

Consider the deified feminine and masculine to be as vast as the cosmos. In seeking out the ways that the pantheon of our great world are ingrained in your sacred work as a Witch, know that there is no need to feverishly memorize each and every name of the major Goddesses and Gods from every culture and every time. It is far better to freely explore the divine realm like the liberated woman you are, resisting cultural appropriation and fearlessly seeking your own frontiers but leading with your heart. Trust in your own path, my love, and much will be revealed to you when the time is right.

Hold steadfast to this truth: The Goddesses of the world are high-energy archetypes that will teach you much about yourself. If you resonate with a particular Goddess or God, it is likely because that deity possesses traits that are integral to your soul's path and embedded within your own body and psyche. Listen for their holy voices, and honor the abundance and fertility of the pantheon.

A *Spirit-Study Practice*

Scholarly Priestess, examine the Goddess deck you have created with your own hands. Can you ascertain any cultural roots for the sacred feminine manifestations you have drawn? If these Goddesses lived as human beings in a particular place at a particular time, where and when would that be? The ways the Goddess has presented Herself to you, as her daughter-student, are valuable clues to where your spirit study should begin. If an actual time and place do not present themselves readily, consider the roots of your Goddess's names, any animal familiars by which they are likely to be accompanied, the landscape in which they live, and any other number of biographical details that will serve as cosmic clues to where your study will begin.

If you find common cultural threads among your Goddesses, begin there! Research the mythologies and histories of civilizations that seem pertinent to your Goddesses, and be open to finding similarities between the Goddesses of cultures that appear too distant, geographically or otherwise, to be affiliated with one another. Remember that the Goddesses are all manifestations of the divine feminine force, and it is the same force that lives inside you. As you explore, surrender to the Mystery as it presents you with the holiest of your soul guides. Be endlessly respectful, but do not feel confined to cultures and religions with which you are most familiar. As your wealth of knowledge expands, you will begin to discern the elements of God and Goddess that are most integral to your way of living as a Witch in the wild world; allow this to happen very organically, for you have not come here to be told what to believe. The liberation of your Witch's soul means you no longer have to conform to the religious practices of others; you now seek and find for yourself.

The Marriage of the Divine Feminine and the Divine Masculine: A Bedtime Story

Once upon a time long gone, this small part of the cosmos we human beings now call our own was inhabited only by divine beings of light; these diamond-energy souls were compassionate devotees to both the sacred feminine and the sacred masculine, and their way of life was bound to the cycle of time. On the eve of the winter solstice, the Goddess who was worshipped so sweetly and fervently by these beings would become pregnant with the God-Child of light; the souls of the world rejoiced as the Goddess's belly swelled with the holy pranic fire of life, and when She gave birth to the very embodiment of the sacred masculine at the vernal equinox, a rowdy celebration was held to which all of nature was in attendance.

As the spring waxed toward the summer season, the roles of the God and Goddess were transformed; the Mother Goddess became younger, a sultry full-breasted Maiden, and the God-Child grew older, a virile hunter God. The relationship was no longer one of Mother and Son but, rather, one of the sacred lovers. The God and Goddess were much in love, as the Goddess infused the God-consciousness with much power and movement. The Goddess made the God manifest in this world, made Him lust after life itself, and the two were entrenched in a summer romance that rocked the whole of the Earth. Orgasmic eruptions of flowers and fruits mirrored the ecstatic partnership of God and Goddess, but autumn was nearing.

As the autumnal equinox approached, the Goddess became saddened and willful, knowing that Her God would soon leave Her. She became the Crone Goddess as the leaves fell, and on All Hallow's Eve, the God passed on to another plane. The Goddess lived in solitude and mourning, until the light returned on winter solstice night and the light-beings saw Her through it all; they saw Her move from Motherhood to Maidenhood to Cronehood and back again, spiraling through time as the great wheel turned through the seasons. Though the sacred masculine leaves the Earthly plane for a few months every year, the sacred feminine stays. She births the whole world into being, and She is steadfast in Her task; it is for this reason She is worshipped.

This traditional pagan mythos has much to teach us about our Goddess nature; it is wild, majestic, and enduring, but never static. The dynamic and mutable holy feminine is nourished by the elements and seasons of our natural world and the most fundamental source of nature's soul-food. Relationships with both the self and others will shape-shift, and the spiral of time will keep moving in its nonlinear but ever-changing dance. A woman must reject the immutable qualities of rigid spirituality, for she is at once the sensual Maiden, Creatrix-Mother, and intuitive Crone. The feminine will not be contained, nor will you.

Verses of the Holy Feminine
In Her Name, We Pray

Our Mother, who art rolling in the ever-loving mud with us here on our Earthen plane, hallowed be thy name. Bless the beauty of our abundant world, fully manifested and wholly graceful. Bless our soul-food and

our abundant harvest. May all those who sit at our table be free to honor their holy sensuality and raw spirit light. May we break bread only with those who care to truly know us, and may we see the union of sacred relationship in all things light and dark. Thy Queen's reign come, and thy will be done, as above so below. Give us this day our daily dose of wolf howls and firelight, and forgive us when we forget the majesty of our feminine being, as we forgive those who carve their wounds out on our skin, if only to remove these shadows from our red, raw hearts. Lead us ever into temptation. May we sip daily from the cup of spiritual and sensual desire, and may we honor our temptations as clues to our soulpath. Deliver us from all cages, those we build ourselves and those built for us, for thine is the Queen's realm, the power, and the glory forever. So mote it be. In Her name, we pray, amen.

Awakening the Feminine Divine
A Feminist Call to the Witch

You may wonder why I have focused so intently, dearest Witch, on the divine feminine while only touching on the invaluable sacred masculine. The wealth of God archetypes holds many gifts for a society starved for spiritual diversity and nourishment for the wild man. Feminist spirituality does not favor the Goddess over the God but, rather, acknowledges that much gender disparity exists in the world's major religions. The Witch is sensitive to patriarchal dominion channeled as the male God, and I will tell you this: Awakening the feminine divine is the most integral part of any feminist agenda.

Men and women alike have been yearning for the succor of the Great Mother, and many of society's ills are inextricably bound to Her imprisonment. The oppression of women has irrefutably occurred as much through misogyny in the name of spirituality as it has through other economic, political, and legal channels. LaSara Firefox writes in *Sexy Witch* that "it is important to recognize that all of us — woman, man, boy, and girl — are trapped in this cultural game." Every gender is served by Her return, and for this reason we must proclaim that we are She. My dear Sister, we have been born into this globalized community of cultural fluidity for a reason, and from the bottom of my Witch's heart, I believe that reason is to bring Her back. A great imbalance exists in our world, with all other populations holding less political, economic, and social power than heterosexual men. Human beings are sensual bodies, creative and emotional minds, and conscious spirits; to deny the role of the feminine in the spiritual facets of our global community is to starve the spiritual dimensions not only of all women but of all humankind.

Every time you honor the feminine divine as part of you, as alive and well inside your psyche and body, a quiver in the energetic web of divinity surrounds us. Every time you give a nod to your Witch's identity and acknowledge the wild within you, we move closer to a pan-gender-equal world. I urge you now to sense the profound truth of the feminine divine's awakening in a world so pervaded with male dominance, and I am crying out for you to set a place for the Goddess at your table.

She needs us, and we need Her. She is us, and we are Her. There is no wall between you and the sacred source, my love, so burn your shame. To embrace your own divinity is not sacrilege; it is your birthright. If you are able to honor the Goddess openly, do so for those who cannot. I am calling you out as a Goddess born as woman, and I am affirming your place in the realm of deity. You, Sister-Goddess, are who we have been waiting for all these Motherless years, and I stand with you as a grieving orphan longing for Her return.

Come to the temple with me, and light candles for Her. Let us show Her we have not forgotten our nature, and let us sing out in unity hymns we were forbidden to learn. Teach your daughters to roll in the mud with you, and teach your sons the merit of their tears. The scent of the charred skin of women burned for their healers' beliefs still hangs thick in the air around us, my love, but do not be afraid, for She is with us. Run with me now into the night fearlessly, and let us bleed onto the ground. I love you, Woman, and we are in this together. Come with me, and let us bring our Mother home! You are a Woman Most Wild, and your global family needs your divinity!

Chapter 8

Prayerful Pathworking and Deep Being

*C*onnection to spirit is cultivated in solitude and silence as much as in circle, ritual, and sacred communion. There comes a time for the Witch to shut out the world and sink into her indigo depths, and she knows this time has come when her intuition is strong, throbbing at her third eye like a tiny diamond-light drum. Much knowledge of the sacred self and one's role in this evolving world can be gleaned from states of deep being and the pathworking that happens there. In these relaxed states of consciousness, the Witch gets a sense of her higher purpose, rationale for her woundings, and a uniquely empowered sense of identity. Having affirmed your own embodiment of God-Goddess-Mystery, now it is time to consider your soul's growth as extending behind and beyond this current life of yours. In this chapter I offer you pathworking experiences through which you can begin to glimpse the ethereal, high-frequency world of Spirit. Many lifetimes you have lived, my love, and a spectrum of spirit guides has walked with you on your path.

A woman is slowly separated from her intuitive self, beginning in adolescence. She learns to deny all that she cannot rationalize in words for fear of being admonished by friends and family. When she closes herself off so completely from her ethereal guides and sacred ancestors, they stop coming to her, even in dreams. The subtle vibrations of the universe will cease writing their holy letters to you if you keep refusing to read them. Should the unheard message be one of weighted importance, integral to her soul's purpose, the Mystery will stop at nothing until the message is received. Very often we will accept only pure, excruciating agony before we finally perk up our She-Wolf's ears, listen, and make the changes our soul demands of us. Keep your intuition turned on and up as often as you can, my love, and you will find that fertile soul support exists in the less visible realms.

THE SOUL WELL MEDITATION

Center your consciousness at your third eye, Wise Woman. Sink into your breath's steady rhythm, and count steadily your next thirteen exhales. Your frequency is rising with every breath you take, and you are joining the realm of the ancients, the angels, and the ascended. Know that as your lungs empty the air from the thirteenth breath, you will be surrounded by a landscape your soul has chosen for you.

Look around you, Pathworker, and see where you have been planted. Perhaps you are in a high-ceilinged temple carved with sacred images. Perhaps you are in a modern home. You may find yourself in the forest or on the ocean floor; it matters not. Whatever your surroundings, begin to make your way toward what looks to be an ancient stone well. The structure is vine wrapped and moss covered, and you can sense its power from where you stand.

Affirm that you are safe and shielded as you move toward the Soul Well in which you will be shown authentic visions of who you have been, who you are, and who you will become. Ask your guides of both spirit and soul to show you a time in your past, in this life or one long gone, when you were living out your soul's purpose. Place your hands on the well's edge, and peer inside to the dark watery depths. What do you see there? Is it a memory still on the surface of your mind, or is it one you have forgotten? When ready, shift your gaze away from the well water and ask your guides to show you a very recent reflection of you living your soul's truth; this one will be familiar and fresh in your mind's eye. Can you intuit any connections between the first vision and the second? Is a common action or feeling associated with the authentic you of your past and that of the present moment?

Finally, ask your guides to reveal to you a future vision of you living out your soul's truth. This is a moment in time that has been designed for you by the Mystery, a moment of great transformation and immense growth. Does the image you receive seem to be situated in this life or a future one? What are you doing? Can you glean any shared threads between this vision and the former two? The Soul Well holds clues both to your unique, sacred purpose and to the future of our human community. The visions you have been shown were those you were intended to see at this moment in your magickal life.

When ready, return to a waking state by counting your exhales, beginning with thirteen and ending with one. When you reach the last breath, you will be fully alert, and you will remember all that the well has shown you. Write down all you have seen in this state of high-frequency consciousness, my love, for there is much to learn from what seems to be a dream. Honor and respect what your guides have shown you, and they will reveal to you much, much more than you can imagine with your smaller mind.

A woman must open herself wholly to messages from the Mystery. You have signed up for the most rigorous training the world has to offer you, and, dear Sister, you must complete every course, for you have paid dearly for this education with all the resources you have. Your guides will support you in this sacred endeavor, and they will be there when you graduate with a doctorate of soul-work on your deathbed.

The realization that the wild world extends into the ether will perplex even the most open mind. Women coming to know this integral aspect of the Mystery must surrender the need to know everything about what their senses are telling them. You must invite the unknown into your bed and then relinquish the need to ever hear from it again. Wild woman spirituality does not promise you total knowledge and all-encompassing understanding; conversely, it will expand your world infinitely, well beyond the safety of what you know for sure. When you are quite certain that you know absolutely nothing, you are standing firmly on the ground of wild spirit.

GIFT OF THE HIGH HEALER
Meeting the One with Hands of Light

The hands of the Witch are hands of magick, dear Sister, and awakening to your role as a healer of our world is integral to your path. Seated with the spine upright, rub your palms together sensually and slowly, building some heat between them, and then rest the backs of the hands on your legs. Close your eyes and begin to feel a pinpoint of white light centered on each of your palms; you may feel this as a swelling tingle, and it may feel stronger in one hand than the other.

Bring your attention to your breath's rhythm, letting every cycle of breath open your energetic pathways. You will now take seven breaths, elongating the spaces between the inhales and exhales. With each inhale, the light in your hands will begin to expand, and with each exhale, the light will grow brighter. At the end of the seventh exhale, you will be filled with and surrounded by the pure white light of the healer, and you will find yourself in the presence of your highest healing guide.

Healing guides are very often represented by the sacred masculine, though not always. Notice all you can about your guide, and envision yourself holding your energetic hands outward toward her/him/it. Let your guide tell you of your role as a healer in this life as well as in your past lives. Your guide may speak of self-healing, global healing, or anything in between. Your guide may wish to offer you a gift that will bolster your healing power, or she/he/it may not. Accept whatever you are given with much gratitude, and bid your guide farewell in whatever way seems appropriate, knowing that your guide is always with you.

Once your guide has left you, bathe in your healing light for a time before coming back to the alert state by counting down from seven breaths to one. Your hands may feel abuzz for a few hours after this meditation; if it is distracting, you can diffuse the energy by putting your hands on the Earth or rubbing some sea salt into your palms.

Know that you are a Witch-Healer, my love, and those who need you will seek you out. Do not run from this role, but do not exhaust yourself, either. Fierce self-care is the healer's sanctuary, and you must attend to yourself before others. Reclaiming the healer archetype is the great work of the Witch. The overwhelming majority of women who were targeted by the Witch-hunts did not call themselves Witches; they were a diverse group who, if they shared one commonality, often resisted the socially acceptable roles of married, financially dependent women. They were midwives, mothers, and medicine women, and they were vulnerable to prosecution for innumerable reasons, not the least of which was the predatory suspicion powerful men had of knowledgeable women.

Women whose souls have signed on to be healers in this life are tasked with a great taking back of all that has been stolen from them. Honor the healing power you hold in your hands and your heart, my love, for it is a world-changing fem-force that cannot be discounted. The healer's power is both lusted after and feared, and the healer archetype's ferocity is often overlooked. A healer is not always mere soft compassion; she often reopens the wound and rebreaks the bone. Be a discerning healer of our wild world, Witch, and know that your time has arrived.

THE ANIMAL OF POWER
Calling In the Wild

As a wild woman, your wealth of spirit and soul guides is not limited to human form. You are a child of nature, and the animal kingdom has much to teach you. Center your consciousness at your solar plexus now, and envision the bright fires of the Manipura chakra; remember, this is the energetic domain of self-esteem, identity, and power. Begin to breathe in a steady, drumlike rhythm, with every inhale accompanied by this inner mantra: *I am*. Your exhale is accompanied by a long, hissed *Wild*.

Every breath is an affirmation of your liberated nature, and when ready you will find yourself surrounded by a natural scene; you may be in the sky or underground, beneath the sea or running in the woodland. Notice the domain of your power animal, and consider what the landscape reveals about your totem's wild nature. With heightened senses, you may hear or smell your power animal first. You may see bits of fur or feathers on the ground before you see the actual creature. When it is ready, your power animal will show itself to you.

Do you know this creature? Does it seem otherworldly or of the Earth? It may communicate in voice or through thought, but ask your power animal to tell you something of your wild nature. Ask your animal for signs when it is near, and ask your animal how you can better serve the creature community.

When ready, begin to breathe with a reversed mantra, citing *Wild* as you inhale and *Am I* as you exhale. Breathe movement into your body, and let the air nurture your most instinctual self. Your eyes will open to find the world in a greater state of clarity, as you see with the eyes of your power animal for a time. You, wild Witch, are a complex web of psychic energies writhing in a body heavy with blood and bone; these energies are connected to the whole of the world around you, lining space and time. Every living creature is connected through this pranic net, and once you have consciously tapped into it, you will begin to receive gifts from Mother Nature as well as other aspects of the divine source.

A woman craves regular and conscious acknowledgment of her primal nature; such a practice is not consciousness lowering but an affirmation of her position in the world. We want, so much, to be both sultry animal and spiritual Queen, but we are regularly told that these two integral aspects of self cannot coexist. Marry your inner animal, my love, snuggle it close, and pray all the while.

Attending the Witches' Council
Meeting the Maiden, Mother, and Crone

As the moon wanes toward darkness, enter this meditation by affirming your intention: You will be taking your seat at the Witches' Council and meeting three of your higher spirit guides. Center your consciousness all the way down at your root, and call to mind the color red. Take three long breaths as you bathe in red light, and then call to mind the color orange. Move your consciousness up to your energetic womb, dearest, and breathe thrice surrounded by the jewel-mandarin shade of your sacral center. Shift your awareness to belly center, and let the fiery yellow light both fill and encircle you. Breathe three hot dragon breaths before lifting your awareness up to heart center, reveling in the emerald-green love light and taking three long breaths. You can feel your frequency lifting as you do this, with your body-mind sinking into a relaxed, heightened state of consciousness. Center yourself now at the throat chakra, breathe with the bright blue-turquoise light, and then bring your awareness last to the third eye. You are now encompassed within a dark indigo energy that is feeding your intuition and soothing any stresses your physical body may have.

At the end of the last third-eye breath, find yourself in a primeval forest. Over your head loom great trees, knotted and ancient, and under your bare feet is the soft loam of the Earth Mother's bosom. Before you burns a modest fire surrounded by four boulders, and you sense that one of these seats is intended for you. The sliver of the silver moon shines above you, offering little light, and you hear them coming long before you see them.

The first being you see is your Maiden guide. Notice all you can about her as she approaches her stone seat. Perhaps she introduces herself to you by name. Your Mother guide is next to enter the scene, and you make note, without judging, who your Mother guide seems to be. Finally the Crone enters. Who is this Wise Woman who has been with you for countless lifetimes? When all three women have taken their seats by the fire, they urge you to join them.

You are in a women's circle of spirit now, my love, so make the most of it. Your guides will offer you much advice if you let them, but do not be concerned if they seem uncompassionate or distant. Your guides want you to know only what you are ready to understand, and they will not answer every question you ask. Their words may be confusing or seemingly off topic, but trust that they know what they are doing. Ask your Triple Goddess guides anything you desire to know in this moment, though know that they may not answer you, and stay with your council as long as you wish.

When ready, offer gratitude to the three women for what they have given you. The Crone will exit the scene first, with the fire dying to just a dim flicker of light. The Mother will leave second, and the fire will be nothing but smoldering red ash. Finally, the Maiden will leave, and you will be left in the dark of the moon's light.

Center your awareness at your third eye and count three breaths within an indigo light. Drop your awareness to your throat center, counting three breaths in the turquoise-blue before three more breaths with your being encompassed in the emerald-green light of your heart. Feel your body and mind awakening as your awareness moves to your solar plexus, and you breathe thrice bathed in yellow firelight. You begin to move your fingers and toes slowly as your awareness drops to your bright-orange sacral center, and you take three breaths there before ending at the red root.

At the end of the third root breath, the red light gives way as you open your eyes. Write down all you remember about your council meeting now, and trust that your Triple Goddess advisers are there for you whenever you need them. Honor them by heeding their words, and affirm the authenticity of your seat on the council.

That you have the fierce support of many beings you have not met in a fully alert state is a daunting realization. A wild woman finds comfort in these unseen forces of spiritual mentorship, trusting that her guides and ancestors have her proverbial back, even if she has not yet learned their names or seen their faces. Welcome a certain level of faith into your life. Honor the processes of both spiritual and soulful growth, and know that the way of the wild woman is one of full-light, divine liberation and much hedonistic, Earthly enjoyment.

Verses of the Holy Feminine
Vows for Protecting the Ethereal Wild

I vow to love, honor, cherish, and protect the messages I receive from the Ethereal Wild. I fiercely affirm my dreamscapes as luscious, information-fertile realms gifting me with nightly blessings and divine clues as to where I must go next in this wild life of mine. I raise my hands in empathic blessing for my Soul-Mothers, steadfast ancestors, and spirit guides who surround me at every moment, granting me a mission, should I choose to accept it. I hereby vow to protect the high-frequency realm as it has chosen to represent itself to me, and I will open my eyes wide to the unseen. So mote it be.

BARE FEET, FIRM ON THE GROUND

Exploring the psychic realm will reveal your world as a many-layered and multidimensional space in which subtle energies coexist with that which is readily seen. Plant your bare feet firm on the ground, my Sister, and resist becoming too consumed by the world of spirit. You are in this human form now for a reason, Being of Light, so do not let your crown chakra become too heavy too soon. Remember, you are the divine feminine in the shape of a human woman. There is a time to soar with the angels, and there is a time to get dirt under your nails from planting things; both hold merit equally in the Witch's way of being in this world. Seek balance in your roots and solace in movement as often as you communicate with your guides in a still-bodied shape. You, grounded Seeker, are truly a Woman Most Wild, and your sacred circle of sisters awaits you.

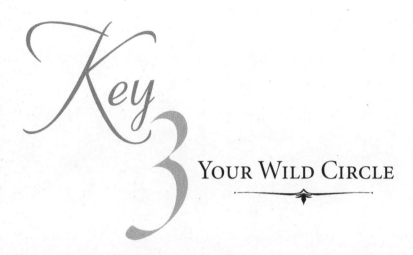

Key 3

YOUR WILD CIRCLE

✦ Invocation

Read to me the holy verses
You scratched in blood on stones
And I will lift the fear-born curses
They used to crack your bones.
Then you leave, and I will, too.
We'll meet again someday.
But don't look back, whatever you do,
Trust the wild woman way.

*O*nly one lock remains on the door, my love, and its key is formed from the sturdy woods of sisterhood and circle-craft. You have been alone in here so long, your Witch's soul screaming to be sprung from the shadows. You have harvested a deep knowing of time's many spirals, and you have remembered your She-Magick. Witch you are, and Witch you have always been. Reclaim wild womanhood now as a way of boldly being in the world, and stand with your feminine bloodline in solidarity. Reject your fear of being seen, and hear the Great Mother's heartbeat quicken as you cast your Witch's light beam far and wide.

Woman, your Sister-Witches are waiting for you to join them; they, like you, are thirsty for a safe place to call their spiritual home. Once that door before you opens, it will be your turn to hold out your hands, to open your heart, and to feel the solace of the circle. I am calling you out now as a Wolf-Woman who can and will find her pack. I am calling you out as a High Priestess who holds every tool she needs inside her womb. I am calling you an eternal student in a world where there are no master Witches, and I am calling you out as an agent of change in a world where women have been robbed of their tribal nourishment. Women need other women. We need to share deeply of our experiential harvest, and we yearn for a space to enact this sisterhood that is both safe and sacred.

Too often the call to circle is left unanswered because our world has pitted women against one another. We are told we must be more masculine in order to succeed, that our femininity is tantamount to weakness, and that our relationships with men are far more valuable than our relationships with other women. The bond that is forged between women within a circle, however, is unlike any other, for it is born of soul and spirit rather than ego. In a true circle, the egos of individuals are minimized if not downright broken apart by the power of the nonhierarchical circle. Whether you are a loud-mouthed extrovert with an enormous global social circle or a woman who needs only a handful of close friends, you will find a particular solace within the circle that cannot be found in a world where most relationships are forged, at least initially, between two egos, two separate individuals whose energetic fields are engaging with one another to create something new.

The traditional coven, just like any type of organization, can be negatively affected by woundings born of hierarchical order. Positioning one individual over another, having to climb the ranks in order to be deemed worthier, has created an unfortunate environment in which the uninitiated ego becomes predator. Younger aspiring Witches especially are struggling to find a spiritual community in which they will not feel less than or, worse, targeted. To them I say create your own community where there is lack. Wild woman spirituality calls you to constantly color outside the lines, to not only break down boundaries but ask why they exist in the first place, and to reject any social structure that jeopardizes your soulful and spiritual health.

The commodification of sisterhood has caused an additional and often overlooked wounding to the women's circle; by this, I mean the often very costly products, workshops, and groups commonly based on the concepts of empowerment and belonging. A proliferation of these business strategies has emerged during recent years, exploiting the very real craving women feel for in-circle communication and excluding large populations of women who cannot afford to participate.

Such channels of consumer culture are creating greater inequality by positioning financially wealthy women in circles of spiritual sisterhood but completely opposing access to such nourishment for those with more limited resources. The creation of a Witches' Circle need not cost anything more than the energies of those who seek to sustain it, and all women deserve authentic spiritual nourishment.

To you I say turn the final key. My Sister, turn the key and let a violet beacon erupt from your crown and into the night, calling all wild women on Earth to come home. Turn the last key, and claim your place at the Witch's round table, for what lies outside this suffocating space you have called the world is the Kingdom of She. My love, hear me when I fiercely affirm the women's circle as a sacred space where the mask falls off, a temple in which bursts of magickal insight explode in the space between thinking and speaking, and a forgotten realm of crafting and communing awaits you. Turn the last key, and come home, for we are all waiting for you.

Chapter 9

The Blessed Magick of Circle-Craft

$\mathcal{A}$ harmonious sort of mystery infuses a circle of women who identify with the call of the wild. The magick of Witches' circle-craft emerges from out of this mystery as a heart-born energy that is raised both spiritually from above and soulfully from below. The souls of the individual women support the circle with strong roots of subjective opinion, unique experience, and personal passion, while the interconnected spirits of the circle members illuminate the circle from above. Both soul and spirit nourish the circle as a sacred and safe space that is nonhierarchical, with these two energies coming together in every woman at her heart center and uniting her with her sisters.

The core difference between a traditional coven and a Witches' Circle is the absence of a linear hierarchy; this is not to say that there are no covens organized in a nonhierarchical structure or that hierarchical covens are in any way dysfunctional. However, the perception of a coven as being shaped and dictated by a religious order, led by a High

Priestess alone or in union with a High Priest, has generated significant resistance to coven membership, particularly in young Witches eager for a safe space to hone their Craft. There absolutely is and has been a role for the traditional Wiccan coven, and I would not discount the beauty or the divinity of these structures as true change agents in our evolving society. In my experience, women feel a unique need for wild, spiritually empowering communion with others that only a nonhierarchical, accessible circle can fulfill.

The Witches' Circle is unique in structure as well as function, with feminine energy bolstered through both deep communication and magick work. The Witches' Circle is already transforming the collective energy of our world by honoring the equitable holiness of every woman born. Coming together with your wild sisters to make magick, communicate authentically, beat drums, weep under the full moon, and cultivate the Creatrix Fire together is not only a game-changing action; it is a fem-force of global transformation. In this chapter I will call you out as a feminine agent of miraculous and mysterious fortitude, and if you are open to the role, you will begin to receive messages from the cosmic web on how to optimally fulfill a Goddess-sanctioned necessity.

Human beings need spiritual companionship. The very nature of spirituality is its affirmation of our interconnectivity. Within our crown chakras resides the universal and energetic validation that we are all *one*; for this reason, a hallmark of wild woman spirituality is circle-craft. In my experience, women absolutely crave deep communication with other women or those who, regardless of gender, embody a strong, feminine energy; these are conversations about the cosmic order peppered with anecdotes about lovers and children. When women speak of their deeper and wilder selves, the divine feminine glows a little brighter within the collective global community.

Many Witches feel much more comfortable as solitary practitioners than as participants in a circle. However, I do assert that we are stronger together. The isolation of women, in its myriad forms, is an instrument of patriarchal dominion, and I hold the Witches' Circle as an integral spiritual technology to our collective future. Mind you, it may well be that you are not drawn to belonging to, much less creating, a Witches' Circle. Should you feel more authentic as a solitarily practicing Witch, know that this is absolutely valid and true for you at this point in your spiritual evolution. You are no less Witch if you are casting strong circles in your kitchen than if you are howling under every full moon with your many sisters. All ways are true, because a Witch is someone you *are*, not something you do. Force nothing. Let it come.

THE WITCHES' CIRCLE
Principles and Absolutes

The Witches' Circle is undergirded by feminine values, absolutes of peaceable, karmic communication, and three fundamental principles that emerge from these symbiotic forces. The overarching principle of the circle is this: No member of the circle is any less worthy than another, regardless of seniority or any other factor that might inform levels of value; such is the feminine way, and women's circles of various types have been forged according to this core ideal for generations. Though the circle can, and in some cases must, have some form of leadership, the leader does not designate herself as holding power over the other members of the group. Consider yourself, my Sister of the Sacred Circle, as a sacred space holder who helps to contain the circle's energy.

A second principle of the Witches' Circle is this: The circle, much like the energetic circles in which you perform your solitary magickal work, my love, has a life of its own. Inside this sacred space, spellcraft coexists with wound work and storytelling, soul growth is just as valued as spirit growth, and voice and silence complement each other regularly and as the circle determines. Consider the Witches' Circle as an emerging and magickal context for decision-making processes, clear seeing, and shared vision as much as it is space for energy raising, divine feminine ritual, and spellwork. Each woman within the Witches' Circle has a unique and wild energy that supports and, much more salient, transforms the overall energy of the circle. The alchemy of the circle's energy is similar to that of a romantic partnership, with the energies of the two souls coming together to form something entirely new; this is in contrast to the typical perceptions of a partnership as pieces coming together. A circle is a holistic entity to which all women are integral, with the circle itself a living, breathing, and changing space that, in a sense, has been designed by the Mystery.

The final principle of the Witches' Circle rests on its sanctity, and it is this: The Witches' Circle is a holy space in which all women are co-creators of a socially just soul- and spirit-centered future. The sanctity of the circle means that communication is heart centered, there is no invalidation of circle members' opinions or beliefs, and there is no denigration of the circle's divinity. When women enter the Witches' Circle, they become keepers of sacred space. Anything spoken or shared within the circle is not discussed without members' permission, not solely out of mutual respect but because what is born inside the circle must be protected with all the ferocity of a wolf mother.

Your circle of wild women is a place where you gather to be soulfully authentic and spiritually connected. Here the ego is dissolved in the name of sacred work and the feminine divine; there is no room for aggression, greed, or selfishness because the circle is energetically full of that which, by definition, is egoless. Such is the sheer magnificence of the Witches' Circle, for conflicts are rare in a place where connection is true. Honor the principles of the Witches' Circle, and, my dearest Sister-Witch, you honor it as the home of the wild spirit.

The Witch's Homecoming: A Feminine Fable

This unapologetic creature had known she was a Priestess for as long as she could remember, but she was taught to fear the ways of the Witch. This woman, so lovely and wise, knew of the magick in her blood, felt the vibrant and orgasmic rush of the seasonal shifts, and secretly kept a stash of spell-casting tools under her bed. As is the path of many brave medicine women, with age came fearlessness for this Wild One.

Perhaps it was a fire spirit who came to her in her dream, or perhaps it was simply the time her soul had designed for her awakening; in the end, it matters not what caused her liberation. One fateful morning, she awoke and no longer cared who saw her bury the spell bag in her yard, heard her chant, or, for that matter, saw her bare rump. No more did she feel society's grip on her heart when she proclaimed aloud who she had known herself to be all those years: "I am a Witch of the White Moon!" she yelled. "I am a worthy Wolf-Woman! I am whole, and I am home!" No longer was this temple dancer trapped by her own rules, and she ran into the dewy dawn a Witch reborn.

She ran out of the house she felt was no longer her own and sought a new home, a soul-home. With senses heightened, the woman could hear her sisters' laughter from miles away. She unpinned her hair and headed for the hills, following the cackles and the guffaws. The whole of the day she sought them out, knowing that any sacrifice — her tired body, her hunger, her loneliness — would be one well made.

Just as her legs could carry her no farther and the full moon was peeking over the tree line, the woman saw the maternal glow of the council fire. Sourcing energy only from their voices, she sprinted toward what she knew would be her homecoming. The Witches did not look as she expected they would; their clothes were rainbow colored and their smiles were genuine. She might have met them at the market or the bank, but she did not. She met them here in a sacred circle where only truths were spoken and all belonged, not out in the world where lies were told and exclusion was rampant. She met them here, in the woods, and their raised hands told her she was the Homecoming Queen.

They welcomed her to their fire and bid her to speak. She told them of her Priesthood, her bliss, and her wounds. She spoke of how a wild child lived inside her bones. She told them how she once communed with the ghost of her grandmother and then told them how sweet her puppy's face was. Yes, this woman spoke of spirit alongside soul, and her newfound sisters listened, fiercely affirming her belonging with expressions of sheer knowing. *I see you*, their faces said. *I see you. I know you. I am you.*

She was nourished by them, and she was nourishment for them. They laughed and wept with her, and they called to the North to strengthen their circle. They discussed their dreams for work and family, and they called to the East to enliven and enrich their circle. They spoke of procrastination and motivation, and they called to the South for its fire to energize their circle. They mused over romance and mystery, and they called to the West to purify their circle. They drank the medicine of sisterhood. They cast spells for a reborn world. They claimed their birthright as the Goddess embodied, and then, as the Witching Hour approached, they opened their circle, bid one another farewell, and merrily parted.

The woman began the long journey back to her house, knowing that it would not feel quite as arduous now, for she had been fueled by the magick of the wild. She had sunk her teeth and nails deeply into the hearty bread of a Witches' Circle, and she had reclaimed her right to be who she was. The whole way home, she grinned at the ease of it all, wondering what had taken her so long to find them. When she returned to her family, she was more *her*. She was *She who is*. She was not a mother, wife, sister, and daughter; she was herself, wild and free. She was soul-spirit-God-Goddess. She was everything, she knew it, and her world was better for her knowing.

A point comes in the life of every wild woman when she feels her spirituality needs a very particular form of nutrition. She begins to run for the hills in search of this mysterious spirit-food, questioning how she could ever find something she cannot define. Just before her legs give out from the searching and after she has been gifted with tiny tastes of what she needs, she finds a grand round table has been set for her. She takes her seat there, feasts with those she would not necessarily even speak to during her everyday goings-about, and leaves with her seams bursting from feminine fullness.

Manifesting a Dream Circle

Sink into yourself, my love, and envision your Witches' Circle exactly as you want it to be. Perhaps you cannot clearly see the faces of your sisters yet, but you can feel the palpable energetic qualities of the circle. Know in your cells that this circle will be birthed, that it will be a space as sanctified as any temple, and trust that your sisters will find you. This circle will be a Ministry of the Wild. This circle will be a place to which you go home to find spiritual nourishment as often as you need, and you can see it, taste it, smell it, hear it, and feel it with all that you are.

Call to mind all you know to be true about your Witches' Circle, and write down the most vivid description you can. When you write or speak aloud your vision, you take the first step in manifesting your thoughts into being. Once it is written, it is no longer only in your head; it has been extracted from the ethereal realm of thought and pulled toward a denser state that is more authentic. Describe your Dream Circle with your words, and you gift greater meaning to your hopes and desires. Consider this action the first step in forging your sacred circle and embracing the bliss of sisterhood.

HEART-BASED COMMUNICATION
Speaking from Spirit and Soul

Though your soul knows well the magick of the Witches' Circle, your thinking mind may be wondering how this sacred space differs from a Saturday evening spent gathered around a wine bottle. The miracle of the circle lies not only in its inherent divinity but also in its communicative energy. Within the circle, the energy flows freely through heart-based communications fed by the souls and spirits of each woman. The ego is a key aspect of soul; it is the mechanism for carrying one's soul-work out into the world. Lying beneath the heart, the ego creates the need for separation and individuality; from here, however, conflicts and judgment are born.

Ascend the ego, speak and listen from your heart chakra, and you will truly envelope yourself in the beauteous magick of a circle. The clearest visions and most profound realizations emerge when a circle of women commune from their hearts. While egos can and will affect the circle, particularly if the women in the circle are acquainted outside the sacred space, it is possible and necessary to guide communication to be birthed from heart. Consider all your unique traits, passions, fears, and power sources as the realm of soul, with your undeniable relationship to Goddess, God, and all things in the realm of spirit; when these two forces come together at the heart, a holistic sense of true and empathic connection begins to permeate the circle.

A group of women who merge to share their stories in this way is no less beauteous or energetically powerful than one that comes together to make magick. The circle *is* magick, because it has no beginning or end; it is a manifestation of the eternal wheel of time to which all souls belong, just as a child belongs to its mother. Joining together in a circle creates an opportunity for every woman to share in something mystical and mysterious, with each circle member keenly aware that she is, in herself, whole while concurrently being part of a greater whole.

Hearing the Heart's Wisdom: Honoring the Sister-Priestess

Your heart is a wellspring of great wisdom, my love, and it speaks in a language foreign to our individualistic tongue. The heart-light illuminates the uniqueness of soul and the interconnectivity of spirit within an emerald-green aura marked by sheer compassion and immense gratitude. Pull your consciousness down to your heart center, wondrous Witch; on your inhale pull spirit down along the right, solar side of your body, and on the exhale lift soul up along the left, lunar side of your body. At your holy heart now beats these two drums, the low bass of soul vibrating under the high-pitched pulse of spirit.

Listen to the wisdom of your heart now by calling to mind a conflict you have had with another woman; she may be your blood, a member of your found family, or a veritable stranger, but let her be someone who has caused you slight or moderate pain in the past. You will feel a squeezing at your precious heart's center now, but instead of letting this pressure have its way with your heart-light, begin to let the heart speak. Begin with these words: *When I think of you, I feel...* If you feel your consciousness drop down toward your belly center, draw it up to your heart again; this is likely happening if you continue to speak words of blame or anger. The heart will speak in the most honest and authentic voice you have. Your heart-voice may well express immense woundings, speaking of disconnection, loneliness, and heartbreak, but remember that such words are all born of love and relationship.

Your heart yearns for relationships of the highest integrity, dear one, and it becomes dis-*heart*ened when its passion for connection is extinguished through any number of hurts. The Witch's heart is prone to betrayal because of the collective wound we share — the masculine betraying the feminine and sending her packing while wars were waged in the name of righteous oppression and ego madness. Every individual heart-wound causes our collective wound to ache under the scar tissue, and we do all we can to silence the vulnerable heart-voice out of fear.

In the Witches' Circle, my fierce Protectress, the stone walls around your heart will crumble, and your ego will want to fight against the un-familiarity of being truly seen by your sisters. Be prepared to feel much resistance to this new way of being in the world and communicating with others, for we are socialized to hide who we are and perceive most of those around us as threats. Speak fearlessly from your heart, and you risk nothing other than illumination. Bring out of the dark all you were taught to hide within the safe space of the Witches' Circle, and let your fellow She-Wolves lick your wounds.

You will operate differently within the context of a sacred circle than you do in your workaday life, and this should be so. Trust the way your soul communicates in this space, its energy rising up and out with long arms grasping for intimate, sisterly connection. In *Circle of Stones*, Judith Duerk asks us to consider how our lives, as women, may have been differ-ent had we the holy solace of a women's circle as we grew, offering us this healing image as a promised metaphor for the circle's potential: "Woman, with a candle lighted to help her keep faith with her own life...a centered presence spreading in concentric circles around her." Circles of women are these round stones, being more and more unearthed every day, that are the primary building material in the Motherland's foundation; dig up as many as you can, haul them to the sacred hill, and light the candles, for in doing so you are welcoming Her home.

Energetic Heart Opening for Raising the True Voice

And now I will say this with all the love I have: Your inclination may be to run from this type of intimate connection as if you were escaping from a shadowy figure in a nightmare. You may not know precisely why, but you know you must high-tail it out of there. This instinct to sprint away from feminine intimacy is often a birth defect of the strong woman, one with which I am still sometimes afflicted, and it is attributable to a great disservice done to you by society. We have learned, dear one, to behave as the spiritually motherless behave. We have learned to keep our hearts closed and protected because to open the heart is to be weak, or so we were told.

We have been told that woman's liberation is inextricably bound to her enhancement of her masculine qualities, and this has robbed her of her right to genuinely connect with her sisters. Women distrust other women largely due to a great social blinding that has caused us to ignore the spiritual connection women share as embodiments of the Goddess. All women share the same stories. All women share the same deep wounds and collective joys. All women are me, and all women are you.

Come to a physical position where your heart center is lifted, such as lying supported on the ground with a large pillow or bolster behind your upper back and head. Take one of your hands, curling it into a loose fist, and give your heart center a slow roll, spiraling out from heart center in a clockwise motion. As you do this, feel your emerald-green light beaming from the front and back of your heart, becoming brighter with every breath. Spiral back to center now, and speak these words: *I call in to my life a connection more intimate than I have ever known, and I invite all beings of this wild planet to do the same. I call in spoken authenticity, truth, and wisdom. I call in power and grace. I call in my sacred circle, and I call to the women of this world to rise.*

Your spirit self is much like a billion-year-old star; it does not need to be seen and admired in order to exist, but its beauty is so majestic, so flawlessly emblazoned with the cosmic map, that the whole of the world misses out on laying eyes on a great, blindingly impeccable *something* if you keep it hidden. Let us look upon your God-Star, Woman, even just this once.

Verses of the Holy Feminine
Ten Commandments of the Wolf-Woman

She returned from her pilgrimage to the wild mountain to find us all waiting for her, our faces caked with holy mud, our Witches' war paint. We held our breaths while the Wolf-Woman took down her hood, uncovering her wiry gray hair and revealing her halo of blue spirit light. She commanded us then, her voice mournfully howling with much guttural grace: "Thou shalt honor both your soul's darkness and your spirit's brilliant light. Thou shalt rage against the machine of injustice and oppression. Thou shalt stand up for your sisters who cannot stand for themselves."

We all rose en masse, some of us holding fists in the air and others cradling our babes. The Wolf-Woman continued: "Thou shalt open your legs to the full moon and let the wild nourish your sacred sexual self. Thou shalt pray to anyone and anything that feeds your spirit. Thou shalt reject any spiritual cage that seeks to contain your untamed and holy being."

Whispers of solidarity droned through the crowd, my sisters hissing breathy affirmations of "Yessss." The Wolf-Woman shed her cloak then, standing in all her naked and wise glory before us, and her body glowed with all the divinity of the distant stars. "Thou shalt know yourself as She-Gods whose bodies contain all the vibrating holy fire of the cosmos. Thou shalt take communion from salty seawater and the hearty whole-grain bread of the feminine. Thou shalt worship your own

*perfect soft body by feeding it, shaking it, and painting it
with the sacred symbols shaped by mother's mud."*

We clasped each other's hands now, knowing the
Wolf-Woman was nearly finished with her wild sermon,
and prepared ourselves for some great life-changing
piece of wisdom to fall from her dry lips. Would she bid
us to come with her in a massive march? Would we be
called to harvest blood lust and bare our fangs in the
name of vindication? From the West, a gust of cold wind
tossed our leader's hair about in all directions, and she
opened her mouth to gift us with her final bit of wisdom:
"Thou shalt honor the fallow times when you are called
to be a lone, restful Priestess as much as you honor the
high-fire times when you rally and rise with your sisters.
Go into the holy dark now, my wild women. I am tired.
Let us nourish ourselves in quiet solitude tonight. Tomorrow we will be reborn."*

THE WAY OF THE WOLF-WOMAN

To my mind, the way of the Wolf-Woman is not one of constant contact
with anyone, regardless of gender. The Wolf-Woman craves solitude as
much as she craves relational connection, and to spend too much time
in either state leaves her hungry. In *Women Who Run with the Wolves*,
Clarissa Pinkola Estés writes, "Among wolves there are no such divided
feelings about going and staying, for they work, whelp, rest, and rove
in cycles." The Wolf-Woman finds nourishment in a lonely forest and
in a sacred circle, but she also is fed by her sacred work, sexual union,
creative endeavors in their vast spectrum of identities, her found family
and her blood family, the kaleidoscope of a cat's eye, and the sanctity of
a home well cleaned. The way of the Wolf-Woman is the way of balance,
feverishly sought and fervently maintained.

The Wolf-Woman has created a life worth living not because of what she does but because of who she openly and freely *is*. She lives in alignment with the seasonal cycles, trusting her place in the world as soul designed just for her. She has moved naturally toward her sacred work and away from that which starves her creativity and counters her life's purpose. She may have few friends, but those she has she loves fiercely. She does not apologize for being a woman who many would call "bitch" as easily as they would call her Witch, and she is careful of those to whom her power may be overly invested.

The Wolf-Woman protects herself, cares for her heart and her womb as she would a newborn, because she knows that, in doing so, she is nourishing those sacred, vulnerable parts of every woman in this world. The Wolf-Woman has bled to become who she is, and she shares her wounds with those she deems worthy. She knows that her wounds have made her the Warrior-Priestess she is, and her regrets are few.

The way of the Wolf-Woman is the way of the beast who is both a loner and a pack member, and she oscillates between these roles as she sees fit. She has a deep knowing of her cycles and understands there will be times when she must head for the hills to find her circle or to be alone, and there will be other times when she runs screaming back to her everyday life. The Wolf-Woman has found a way of being in the world that sustains her without overfeeding her or leaving her famished, and she finds magick in that which is outwardly dull and mundane as well as glittery and glamorous. Find the part of you that *is* her, and your circle will come to you. You, dear Sister, are a Wolf-Woman Most Wild, and your pack awaits.

*C*hapter *10*

The Witch's Medicine and Midwifing the Circle

*I*f you begin seeing through the yellow eye of instinct in your belly and the indigo eye of intuition between your brows, you will notice that circles occur everywhere in the She-Kingdom of Mother Nature. Circles are organically formed with no beginning to their border and no consequent end; they are feminine shapes reflecting our inherent wholeness. We will see that the cells in our bodies communicating in electric pulses, the petals of a rose as they unfold, the scalloped shells licked by ocean waves, and countless other reflections of the Holy Round permeate our world, if we choose to open our circle-within-a-circle eyes. When you communicate in a circle, my Sister, you experience a tried-and-true method for enhancing the feminine energy that naturally occurs in our world. In this chapter I offer you a lunar cycle metaphor for the circle's birth, fruition, and surrender, and I ask you to become your circle's caring midwife.

The Witches' Circle provides a safe space for magickal exploration, wisdom sharing, and cocreation that permits every woman to truly be herself, that is, a woman among sisters who has finally found her Red Tent. Sisterhood medicine contained within the circle is magickal in and of itself, but to use the sacred space for Witches' work renders it that much more powerful. Do not be too concerned with ensuring your circle's perfection, for the circle's foundations are those of perfect love and perfect trust. At the crux of your work, wild Witch, is loving the energetic vibrations surrounding you, rising to support you in your evolving way of being in this world, and then trusting that all is coming as it was always meant to, in just the right time and form.

Of course, a perfect circle of wild women may already exist for you. Finding an already existing circle may be easier than creating one of your own, but should access to an existing sacred space feel impossible, do not rule out the possibility of midwifing your own Witches' Circle. Do not question your worthiness now, for fear will whisper loudly that more training is needed, more study, more mentorship. I am an eternal student as you are, my dear, and I believe in continual learning and the rejection of mastery. However, do not let your lack of confidence keep you from walking your soul's path. You are not, after all, seeking to be worshipped; you are claiming your birthright as a member of a wild woman's circle. Know the difference between declaring religious superiority and cultivating a circle; the former is driven by power hunger and the source of this world's greater injustices. You, as the creatrix of a magickal circle, are effectively acting to dismantle the structures built by the aggressive masculine ego. In many ways and quite ironically in a world where women's communion has long been demonized, to create a sacred circle where women share, shake, and spellcast is to oppose the evils of this world.

Begin with a vision for your sacred circle, and be open to receiving gifts sent from the divine feminine Herself. You are not alone in this, and this is weighted work you do. If you have never belonged to a women's circle — that is, a nonhierarchical space in which every woman's words and intention were honored and egos were minimized through careful and compassionate communication — then recall a time when you conversed with someone in a very feminine way. Perhaps it felt as if the language being shared was taking on a life of its own, or perhaps you came to know this other person in such an authentic way through just the briefest of conversations; whatever shape this interaction took, remember the feeling of transformation that followed. Circles are healing spaces of change in which all members are affected by the self-contained miraculous entity that is the circle. You must begin by acknowledging that the circle is truly valuable, as if it were an alchemist's salve for our collective wounds not only as women but also as human beings born into this pivotal time.

A woman mothering her sacred work in the world is challenged to overcome deep indoctrinated beliefs about aggressive goal setting, deadlines, and control; this is not to say that no time or place exists for masculine left-brained order and linear direction, but such a mentality must coexist with the feminine ability to create organically and receive openly the gifts the universe sends. Do not rush circle creation if you feel you are moving against the currents, and do not force something into being whose time has not yet come. You will know when the time is right, my love, because you are listening to the wild whispers so keenly and with much good intent.

New Moon Energy
The Five Spirals of the Circle's Birth

You now know the new moon's energy as intense, lunar fuel for manifestation and the endeavors of sacred work. As the circle begins to form, know the perfect imperfection of this sacred shape's manifestation in nature; there will be hiccups in the plan, and you will know how to handle them when it is time. Harvest the new moon's energy, and begin to articulate a vision for your circle. Be specific, and be pure of intent. Anything that bubbles up from your Witch consciousness is worthy of acknowledging, even if it seems useless or silly. You have already brainstormed a description of your Dream Circle, but now, *now* my dear Sister, it is time to streamline your vision by asking yourself five pivotal questions, the answers to which will become the Five Spirals of Birth for your circle.

Begin to midwife your circle's birth by sitting at the center of a room before a lit candle. If you can, perform this birthing ritual on the day or evening of the new moon. Now ask yourself this: If your whole circle of sisters is upheld by a single deeply held conviction that you all share, what is it? Another way of posing this question to your feminine psyche is this: If you could have the opportunity to share a single sentence with everyone alive in the world today, and they could all truly hear you, not obey you but *hear* you, what would that sentence be? This is the initial Spiral of Intention, and this early labor stage is pivotal to the circle's birth process. In completing this first spiral, you have already laid the foundation for your circle's creation, and the wild feminine is already listening. Move clockwise around the candle once now, spiraling out so you find yourself farther away from the candle when this first circle is complete.

The second spiral is the Spiral of Vision. You may reference your Dream Circle notes for this second labor stage, but now you will articulate, verbally or in writing, how many women you are looking for in your circle. Traditional covens are nine or thirteen, but you are creating a sacred Witches' Circle that differs in structure and intent from a coven. If you want to keep your circle small and allow it to evolve, beginning only with three or four other women, do it. Listen to your womb-voice. Perhaps you want to have an open circle where women can enter and leave the circle freely and as they wish, with no obligation to attend all meetings. My advice to you, Sister, is to begin with the flexible structure that feels the most comfortable and allow it to evolve from there. Most of my circles are open circles where any woman is free to attend, permitting that she knows herself to be open-minded and wild; undoubtedly, these two terms mean different things to different people, but they are two gates that have served me well in my work. In completing the second spiral, ask yourself this: When you see the circle meeting, what does it look like? Once answered, you may spiral a second time around the candle, moving farther away.

The Spiral of Function comprises the third labor stage, my love, and by now you may be buzzing with anxiety, excitement, anticipation, or all three. The Spiral of Function is a practical one in which you consider how you will gather your circle members, express your circle vision clearly and truthfully, and counter any obstacles you foresee to the circle's fruition. Perhaps you already know who will be in your circle; even if you only know of one other woman, she may know someone who may know someone, and the circle evolves in this natural way. Who shares your sacred vision for your circle, my love? If you do not know of anyone, call your circle in by verbalizing it to the universe. Demonstrate your craving for sisterhood medicine, and She will hear you. How often will you meet? When? Where? How will the circle sustain itself? If circle members will be hosting and providing food, should a donation be taken? This third spiral will naturally lead you to the fourth, so when these questions have been answered, take another mindful walk around the candle.

In considering the fourth spiral, you may feel a static electricity in your belly or a throbbing at your third eye; this is the Mystery showing itself to you. The Spiral of Magick is the time to consider how much you want to infuse the ways of the Witch into your circle. Perhaps you desire for spellcraft to be at the heart of your circle. Perhaps you are more interested in celebrating or marking the solar and lunar rhythms. Perhaps you hope only to validate the wildness at the heart of every circle member. Any and all of these intentions, my love, are world changers. Ask yourself this question: What role will magick play in this circle? In answering, complete the fourth spiral, and move onto the fifth and final stage of your circle's birth.

Last, the Spiral of Fem-Fire will fuel the circle's formation and, once finished, the circle will be brought out of the shadows of mere thought and into the light of being. Ask yourself this: What are four things you can do, two a week until the moon is full, to see this circle come to fruition? You may need to make some calls, start a group on social media, clean out that room in your house for a meeting space, or take other practical steps that require motivation. Articulate your four goals now, my love, and get this circle to open its eyes. You are the midwife of this sacred space, but once you have drunk the sweet tea of the sacred circle, you will feel that you belong to it rather than it to you. Complete the last spiral now and, from a distance, stare into the candle's light. Affirm the circle's worth as a change agent in the global community, and silence the small voice that tells you of the circle's unworthiness. Consider yourself now a Witch-Mother, and trust that the circle is growing just as it should.

FULL MOON ENERGY
Circle Meetings and Space Holding

To my mind, the bare bones of a Witches' Circle are enough to begin; these are the energy of the women themselves and a single sacred object that can serve both as the center of the circle and as the talking totem. Do not feel you need to have a well-stocked herbal cabinet, library, or magickal toolbox before you start. You are all the magick you need. For your first meeting, come together as close to the full moon as possible, and introduce the circle's topic; there are recommendations for circle topics in the appendix, but consider the knowledge of lunar and solar rhythms that allowed you to open the first lock to the broom closet.

If the circle's topic aligns with the external rhythms of the natural world, it will most likely speak to the souls of your sisters. You may open the meeting by passing burning herbs clockwise or having the women take a few breaths in unison; the ritual of your meetings will evolve over time, and you need not have it all figured out in the beginning, my love. Perhaps read a passage from a book that speaks to your Witch's heart or pose a question to the group, then pass the talking totem clockwise; this allows every woman to introduce herself as she would like to be seen at that moment, sharing as much or as little about the introduced topic as she would like. Remember, only the woman who is holding the talking totem will speak; there is no interruption unless absolutely necessary.

You, as the circle's creatrix, are a space holder for the feelings, words, and wisdom of every woman in the space, and this can be a challenging role. Sitting in a circle of women is very often an emotional homecoming that brings attention to never-healed, long-forgotten wounds, triggers a dying ego's potentially volatile reaction to its defeat, and creates an opportunity for every woman's most authentic voice to be heard. In essence, it is a space like no other, and a space holder is needed to be the circle's touchstone and boundary maker. In this initial turn around the circle, you will empathically sense both every woman's desire to be a part of the circle and her resistance to such unfamiliar soulful security. This initial sharing cycle is integral to the circle's sustenance, for it marks an initiation; it is every woman's affirmation that they have a right to be there and be heard, and this, in itself, is a powerful and penetrating knowing.

The heart of the circle meeting will lie in what occurs after this initial breaking open, and it may include some initial journaling or partner work in preparation for circle-casting and spellcraft. It may be more of a story sharing or spiritual learning circle than it is a space for actual magick work. Perhaps the women in your circle have agreed to pursue a solitary Witch's path for a time, coming together to share their experiences. The circle is a space for honoring each member's path as her own, and she is always in full agency of her own will and words. Trust that every woman will get precisely what she needs out of every circle meeting, with the energy of the moon illuminating the circle's role in the grander design.

Finally, as the circle meeting winds down, whether or not a magickal circle for spellwork has been cast and open, you will need to afford each woman closure as she leaves the sanctity of this space and returns to her everyday world. You may pass the herbs counterclockwise now or have a closing chant or breath ritual. If the circle has been mostly guided, perhaps permit each woman another chance to speak about how she is feeling as the meeting concludes. Very frequently, the circle ends with a feeling of fullness; this is like a grateful but heavy weight that slowly releases as you leave the circle space. The transformation birthed by the circle will take time to absorb and integrate into each woman's life, and it will do so in very different, personally relevant ways. Trusting that the work has been done and knowing that the circle will be there with open arms when they need it are the tasks of circle members. Your work, my Sister, is to listen to the circle's call to evolve, to surrender to your role as space holder and guide, and to honor your own desire to be a lone Wolf-Woman when the circle energy does not serve you.

WANING TO DARK MOON ENERGY
Support and the Void

Whether the circle meets weekly, monthly, seasonally, or annually, the dark moon spaces between meetings are valuable times when members spiral back into their everyday lives, integrating the magick and the beauty of the circle's miracles into the mundane; these are the times when the overworked Mother finds solace in the memory of her Sister-Witch's words or the lonely Maiden gains confidence from her circle's support to make that call, apply for that job, or leave that relationship. This waning energy demands a necessary surrender from circle members who may crave the nourishment of the circle before the next meeting; it is an energy that must be both relished for the sustenance it provides and respected for its fertile darkness.

As the circle's space holder, my love, stay in tune with this between-meeting time without feeling burdened by it. If you find yourself feverishly planning for the next meeting or reaching out to keep the group together in a way that is not serving your soul, it is time for you to step back and revisit the circle's vision. A circle with strong foundations requires this time to reinvigorate itself before the next meeting, and, depending on your precise role as the circle's founder, you require this time for your own self-care. The greatest piece of advice I can offer you when leading a circle of Witches, Sister-Priestess, is this: Listen to the rhythms of the world around you with your womb-ears, and allow the circle to unfold as a flower bud blooms. There is something mystical about the circle's growth and evolution that can only be described as the beauteously, unpredictably flawless technology of the feminine.

Use this dark moon time to again run as a lone and wild creature runs, for you crave solitude as much as sisterhood. Consider the Witches' Circle a necessary nourishment that feeds you just as it is meant to, precisely when it is meant to; no more, no less. Harbor a constant knowing that the circle does have a life of its own, and, while you and the other circle members are integral to its being, there is an aspect to the circle that is as dynamic and uncontrollable as Mother Nature Herself. I have seen circles birthed, rise full and strong for months or years, and then wane quite naturally and often suddenly; there is a feminine quality to this swelling and thinning, and you may find you are called to midwife your circle's decline as you were its birth. The medicine you drink to ease the loss of the circle is your own holy solitude and the fierce trust that your circle will swell again, if only in a different form, time, and space. You are a driver of the new feminine paradigm, and your wild woman spirituality manifests in your solitary work as well as in your circle of sacred sisters.

Verses of the Holy Feminine
A Blessing for Sealing the Circle

We take each other's hands now to affirm our wild sis-terhood. Our collective heart-drum beats for all woman-kind, and we will still move to this primal rhythm when we are not together. Our souls are bound by the great red cord of trust and devotion, and when we feel lost we will follow its scarlet line back home. These bones are mine. (All repeat.) This blood is mine. (All repeat.) This body is mine. (All repeat.) From my heart to our hearts to the great beating heart of the Creatrix, all blessings be.

THE WITCH PACK

The cycles of within-circle and without-circle time will become gently apparent, very often shifting with the seasons. Remember that your identity as a Witch is entirely your own to claim; it is not sourced from your membership in or leadership of a circle. You were born a wild creatrix, and your memories from childhood are proof of this. You felt more you as a young girl when you were in nature cooking mud pies and running with fern wands than you did when you were screenbound or otherwise stationary. You will belong to a Witches' Circle as your soul intends for you, and your way of being in the circle space may not match that of other women, nor is it meant to. My love, in a sense the circle is a reminder, embedded into your life, of the divine feminine's return. In the faces of your sisters, you will see Her eyes, lined with immense gratitude and the sheer hope for a better world. I weep when I call you a Woman Most Wild, for these words are louder than the dusty death rattle of the outmoded structures of oppression that would tame you.

Chapter 11

The Wild Council
and Pack Life

$\mathcal{T}$ he bridge between the traditional women's circle and the coven is built from the raw mud bricks of wild woman spirituality. The evolution of the circle has no clearly cut trajectory, and it is unlikely to be either predictable or steady. Know that your circle's evolution *is* perfect regardless of how dynamic and changeable it seems to be at any given moment. I am calling on you, Wolf-Woman, to permit the circle to grow as it will but to allow the sacred space to be grounded and molded by natural rhythms. In this chapter I will offer you suggestions for space holding through ritual practices and the magick of Witches' council work. At the same time I urge you to view these suggestions as paint colors on a palette; you should pick and choose whatever works for your circle and aligns with the collective vision of your sisters, and leave out the suggestions that seem ill fitting.

The constants of the circle, despite its fluid attributes, will be maintained by you and your Witch-Sisters. You will begin to trust the vows, both spoken and silent, of the sisterhood, and you will see how naturally the circle aligns itself with the feminine cycles of the Earth. I encourage you to feel into circle-craft as a sculptor feels into her clay; spiral through an intuitive and alchemic practice of seeking, finding, being, and then seeking again, affirming that those in the circle are sharing in these same waves of transformation. Life is change, my love, and the Witches' Circle reflects these consistent realities of ebbing and flowing in time with nature's wheel. As women we are attuned to these rhythms on a womb level, and there is magick in this deep-seated knowledge we all share.

The needs of the circle, remember, are much the same as the needs of the wild woman. The circle needs to feel its place within the natural world, to have it affirmed regularly, and to work its magick. The lifeblood of the circle is the spiritual bond between the women who attend to it, and the ritual of circle-craft arises from the wellspring of their collective intent.

RITUAL OF CIRCLE-CRAFT
Wild Work Lessons

In crafting the Witches' Circle, you will develop a flexible ritual for the meetings themselves that is born out of the shared vision for the circle. The circle's foundations will be decided and affirmed, ideally, by those in the circle; these are the fundamentals of name, identity, core values, goals, membership, communication patterns, and meeting times. Beyond these basics, the ritual of the meeting becomes a sanctuary of sorts, as both you and your sisters begin to trust the cycle of the meeting; you will become attuned to the cycles of silence and speaking, mystical magick work and mundane sharing of the day-to-day, and the energy's waxing and waning. You will trust that the nourishment arising for you during the meeting is precisely what you required in that moment, knowing that it may not at all match the nourishment you are given at the following meeting. Honor yourself, your sisters, and the circle as symbiotic layers of pack life that are both whole unto themselves and deeply influential of one another.

There is no typical circle, and the demystification of the Witches' Circle is essential to its role as a global change agent. If you are able, show the world the beauty of wild women coming together to affirm their spiritual fortitude and collective power. Show your red, raw soul to anyone who cares to see it. Proclaim your sensual divinity to all who will listen, and invite your circle of sisters to do the same, fearlessly feminine and unapologetically wild.

First, a Dream Vision: Witches of the Wildfire

Gathering in the home of the youngest Sister-Witch, the circle of nine sits on sari pillows and batik tapestries; they are in the quiet basement, surrounded on all sides by cool, sweet Mother Earth, and the spring moon beams milky light through the high windows. The candles have been lit, and the ceremonial drinks have been poured. The nine have not seen one another for several weeks, and there is much to discuss about love, grief, joy, nightmares, bright light, and dark shadow. When the time comes, the circle's guide sets down her glass of honey mead and raises her hands high, motioning the others to do the same. She speaks words affirming their identity, the sanctity of the circle, and the evening's intent: *Welcome, sisters! We are the Witches of the Wildfire, and tonight we will work the magick of manifestation for our collective health and well-being. We will respect the divinity of each of our sisters, and we will express our spiritual and sensual freedom.*

The circle guide reads a poem that sparks the She-Fire in the circle; it taps into the primal feminine understanding of the elements and brings tears to the eyes, along with belly laughter. She passes the talking stick to her left when the reading is finished, inviting her sister to take a deep breath and then share. As she speaks, she trusts her sisters will hear her authentically and intimately, perhaps nodding and raising fists in solidarity but refraining from verbal interruption. She speaks of her struggles as a young single mother, and her hopes for her daughter, and she offers gratitude for the circle's safety. In passing the talking stick to her left, the young woman dries her tears and listens as the wise elder seated next to her recalls memories of challenges similar to her own, offering the advice to feel into the pressures of the day-to-day by acknowledging that only presence and the enduring spirit are real. The stick moves around the circle thus, offering every woman a chance to affirm that she is *there*, whole in her body, mind, spirit, and soul.

The circle guide then discusses the magick of manifestation, inviting her sisters to invoke a deeper understanding of what may be next for them on their soul's path. Together, these wild Witches consider complex questions regarding their life's path as sensual creatrixes and begin to fashion spell bags for the purpose of manifesting these admirable wishes. Someone acknowledges the feminine collective's purpose in this moment, as to support their own soul-work in order to cultivate a better human community, and these words spark an epiphany in another sister's psyche. The circle flows like rainwater over muddy ground, carving out new rushing inroads as well as tiny pools of resonating energy that remain long after the downpour of feminine communal energy has ceased.

The members of the Witches' Circle are both rainmakers and reservoirs, washing and being washed by the circle's energy and being wholly and irrevocably changed. When the time comes, the Priestesses cast a collective circle, raising energy to bless their spell bags, each sister's desires and passions amplified by those around her. The sisters chant *As I will, so mote it be!* as the drum beats and the rain stick rattles, and the sphere of feminine vibration begins to expand. When ready, the nine open the circle and send the residual energy above their crowns and below their bare feet. The circle is open, and the spell bags are charged.

The circle begins to wind down, and the mood lightens. Again the talking stick is passed, this time widdershins, or counterclockwise, and each sister is encouraged to share how she feels now, having been a part of the collective magick. One of the Witches cites her physical fatigue amid psychological empowerment, while another offers only a single word when her turn comes: *surrender*, and her sisters understand. The spell has been cast, the energy surrendered, and attachments released. The circle closes, finally, with the guide's reading of holy words, sanctified at the circle's creation and affirmed at the culmination of each meeting: *We, the Witches of the Wildfire, have met merrily beneath Mother Moon. These energetic wombs are ours, centers of death and birth. These spirits are ours, crowns of enduring and deep being, and these hearts are ours, bridges between soul and spirit built of sacred relationship, compassion, and feminine knowing. We are whole. We are Soul. We are one. All blessings be!*

And Now, the Ritual of Meeting Merrily: A Triple Goddess Metaphor

The ritual of the actual meeting occurs in a relatively predicable life cycle. Visible phases of coming together are similar to birth, initial sharing similar to adolescence and young maidenhood, with the ritual's sacred work indicative of mature and generative adulthood, or the Mother phase of the Triple Goddess. Finally, when the circle begins to wind down, an immense wisdom bubbles out of the Wise Elder phase of the meeting.

When the sisters gather together and take their seats in a circle, a settling in occurs in the Witches' psyches; this is a pivotal moment in which all members feel a communal transition away from their individual and separate ways of being in the world and toward that of the feminine collective. The circle's guide midwifes this birth by offering a "fire-starter," or an initial reading, wise words, or even a visual image that reflects the circle's topic. Each of the sisters' opening responses to the reading or other declarations of presence are integral to the process of breaking open, in which the circle erupts into being, like a rose suddenly blooming; each of the circle member's words offer a particular hue or shape that begins to define how the circle will *be*, in that moment, on that sunlit day or moonlit night.

The movement from the Maiden to the Mother phase is initiated only after all sisters have spoken; now, the circle guide will dig a little deeper and describe the true work of the circle. Very often these are questions or topics that would have been too heavy to discuss at the circle's onset, but, having reached a certain level of maturity, the circle is now ready to move on to spellwork. This is the "wildfire" stage of the circle during which the greatest transformation occurs, the energy is raised to its highest and hottest, and the circle, often seemingly of its own volition, begins to contain an alchemical change. There is less of an individual focus and much more keen attention to the collective purpose of the circle. All members become mothers of the circle, their sisters, and themselves, and emotions may run high during this stage as egos cling to the known and the familiar. It is during this stage that the circle is deep in the fire element; circles are cast, councils held, magick created, and change invoked.

In moving away from the Mother phase and toward that of Wise Elder, the wildfire begins to die out as the circle is opened and a reclamation of renewed individuality occurs. At this stage, each circle member becomes a reborn form of herself, having been uniquely nourished by the raw power of sisterhood. Profound realizations occur during this final "ashes" stage of the circle in which every participant knows herself as a holy, hooded phoenix with the face of a knowing Crone. Each circle member has another chance to speak, to articulate how she feels in the moment, and, very often, to offer gratitude to her sisters for their gifts, to the circle as a whole, and to the wild feminine for being present during the meeting.

THE GODDESS COUNCIL
Circle-Craft for Personal and Collective Change

The Goddess Council represents a unique type of circle format in which the wildfire stage of the meeting is composed not of circle-casting and spellwork but instead of a sacred council purposed by either individual or collective transformation. Each woman in the circle will take on a particular role and then adhere to that role as fully and objectively as possible. Goddess archetypes are useful to respectfully designate the council members' roles, but you may use other titles as you see fit.

The council is useful at transformative points in the solar year, such as at the change of seasons, or when a member is in need of collective support and space holding. You may wish to acknowledge that any woman in your circle may call a council meeting when she needs one, or you may want to limit the potential councils to one per season.

During the council, the members of the circle must, to the best of their ability, meet the challenge of forgetting all they know about the council's subject; only what she brings to the meeting can be taken into consideration. For instance, if a woman's council meeting was called in order to address her sacred work, council members cannot introduce information about the woman's relationship, responsibilities, or other issues unless these points are specifically introduced by the council's subject herself. Here I want to note that this nonjudgmental and compassionate aspect of the council distinguishes it from an everyday gathering of friends at the coffee shop. The formality of the council meeting ensures that the process is truly perceived as sacred soul-work, a context in which pivotal decisions are made, crossroads are left behind forever, and long-lost pieces of the self are excavated from the depths of the psyche.

The woman for whom the council is being held should be designated as someone who reflects soul-heart-spirit transformation. Please note that while I am offering Greek Goddess archetypes as examples, you should not feel limited to these. It is important that the Council members' names resonate with them, so any title that feels inauthentic should be avoided. The Aphrodite archetype represents passion, love, and high-fire evolution, so her name works well for the woman who is the subject of the council. Other roles played by the council members should encompass the complexity of the feminine psyche; A Mother Goddess such as Hestia or Demeter can rule over the fundamentals such as abundance, money, and other resources, as well as home and partnership; she is concerned with the root chakra elements of Aphrodite's world and works to ensure that they are protected as needed. Choose a Dark Goddess archetype such as Medusa or Hekate to be concerned with the destruction of all that no longer serves Aphrodite and wants to remove obstacles to her freedom, particularly those formed as outmoded identities and roles. The creatrix, perhaps named Artemis, desires for Aphrodite to take on her true soul-work as sensually and creatively as possible, while Athena is practical, concerned with Aphrodite's healthy boundaries and concrete goal setting. Other roles, depending on how many sisters you have, include the Triple Goddess, the embodiment of the divine feminine and She who desires Aphrodite to acknowledge her inner sanctity; the Soul-Seeker, who wants to be sure that Aphrodite is being true to the life her soul designed for her; Hera, who is honoring sacred relationship and the warrior woman spirit; and Persephone, who is concerned with cycles of death and rebirth within Aphrodite's life. Choose the roles that suit the council's intention, ensure that each council member knows what her role is, and then proceed by allowing Aphrodite to open her council.

All council members should feel they can harvest their own role from within; therefore, it may be most appropriate for the council members to name themselves. I use Goddess names in my councils in order to acknowledge the role of divinity both in the work as well as within every woman. Taking on a name other than one's own additionally ensures the objectivity of the circle's communication. When you are asked to embody the qualities of a Goddess, the language you use is not entirely your own, and you will find that the wisdom you gift as a council member pours from your lips like some sweet and holy wine tapped from the heart itself.

Short Council Form

The shorter council form takes approximately thirty to sixty minutes, depending on how many members are present and how long each woman speaks. If time is very limited, you may need to predetermine that each council member talk for five minutes or less; this ensures that the communication is succinct and truly objective, serving the council's subject instead of the egos of council members. Talking totem in hand, Aphrodite, or the woman for whom the council is being held, will articulate her particular issue or challenge. She will provide only the information she wants the council to consider, and any outside knowledge about her life must be left outside the meeting space. She will then pass the talking totem to her left, where Hestia, or the root holder, sits; Hestia is allowed to ask Aphrodite a single question and then offer her final advice pertaining only to her areas of concern before passing the talking totem to her left; this is the same format for all other council members' turns. The stick is then moved around the circle and returned to Aphrodite, who will discuss everyone's points and make her final statement, as preceded by the following: *In honor of my sacred soul's purpose, I close this council with these words…*

Long Council Form

The longer council form can take two hours or longer but allows for greater interaction between the council's subject and the other council members. Beginning in the same way as the shorter form, Aphrodite, the woman for whom the council is being held, will voice her issue before passing the talking totem to her left. The first time around the circle, each council member is allowed to ask Aphrodite three questions, recording her answers. Aphrodite may add anything she wishes when the stick returns to her the first time. During the second round, the council members offer their advice, and Aphrodite again states how she is feeling when she receives the stick at the second round's conclusion. Finally, the stick is passed a third time, and the council members are allowed to respond to Aphrodite's words, along with those of their fellow council Witches. Finally, Aphrodite closes the council, making her final statements of motivation and transformation.

The feminine council facilitates great clarity for all who sit at this round table; we Witches all have a dire need for decisions, personal and otherwise, to be informed by a council's communicative magick. Calling on a council, as I did when I was pondering the right direction for this book, requires you to surrender your queenly crown for a time. A degree of humility is required when you invite others to weigh in on your sacred work, relationship, and any other issue that demands the objective input of a well-structured council. Women, when seated in council, harvest new understandings and long-buried perspectives from their own heart-soil, gifting their abundance to others only when asked. The way of the council is the way of pack life; you are fully present when called to be, when your particular Wolf-Woman ways are needed, and then you leave to roam alone.

Verses of the Holy Feminine
Prophecy of the Round Table

I have seen a world where decisions are made at round tables shaded by Mother Trees. Here all beings sit together in these sacred spaces of objective discussion and feminine communication, and the table's foundations have been poured with the universal values of sustainability, equality, and environmental consciousness. The Witches have risen, the reckoning has come, but there has been no rapture. We are all still here. Our human hearts beat in unison for our global community's redemption, for the sufficiency of all, and for the freedom to be whole in our sensual, emotional, and spiritual bodies, born of light and dark. All is coming. As the moon of our civilization waxes, all is coming.

THE MERIT OF BELONGING

Undergirding circle-craft is the continual recognition that women are powerful agents of change and space holders for sanctuary. The precise topics of the circle meetings are afforded meaning not only by the external natural rhythms but by the creative She-Magick energy of the women in the circle. Moreover, the meetings of your Wild Wolf Pack serve as regular affirmations of your Witch's identity as situated within the greater context of the feminine divine. When you engage in meaningful, nonhierarchical, and compassionate communication alongside magickal work, you are actively situating wild woman spirituality within the collective global community. Do not discount the merit of sisterhood, Wolf Woman, for it will never undervalue your power. Women who have relinquished their wildness in the name of social belonging experience a profound rebirth when the sacred, majestic traits they suppressed so fervently in order to avoid rejection become uncaged. You, Woman Most Wild, are she who roams the forest naked and free, and your Witch-Sisters continually reaffirm your right to do so, even when society tells you to go home and lock your door.

Chapter 12

Benediction of the Liberated Wolf-Woman

*S*o wide our eyes have opened, my love. So thunderous are our heart-beats. Our collective liberation is so close I can see the silhouettes of our sisters on the horizon, their backs warmed by a blood-red setting sun, their arrival marking the final days of the uninitiated masculine's rule. By uninitiated, I refer to the aspects of the masculine that are not sacred but aimed at dominance and driven by power hunger. The uninitiated feminine, similarly, is directionless and unconcerned with global spiritual connection. When the ego acknowledges the reality of the soul and spirit, the initiation begins, often quite painfully. We are a feminine collective building a sacred world, and your spiritual liberation, Sister, is the strongest load-bearing pillar in this new global community. Honor your part in the human awakening, my love, for it is formidable. Know that every woman in your matrilineal line stands with you when you are asked to defend your spiritual choices, and know that not everyone in your world may understand your path. This final chapter fiercely affirms both your worth as a wild woman and your need for continued nourishment. We are eternal students who are not seeking mastery, and there is no highest-ranking Priestess in this global coven we are birthing together.

NO TURNING BACK NOW, WITCH

Wild woman spirituality has not, and indeed will not, evolve linearly; it is an organic force of nature as unpredictable as a windstorm or a forest fire. The challenge you must now meet is to trust that your Witch's soul will hold a lantern for you when the darkness gets too thick, when others shun you out of ignorance, and when part of you wants to run screaming back into the quiet security of the broom closet. Listen for the whispers of the divine feminine when your ego-voice doubts your choices so loudly that it drowns out your most authentic wisdom, and hold steadfast to your wand when they tell you that magick is meaningless.

Knowing the liberating beauty of living in tune with nature's rhythms, casting circles for spellwork, and cultivating sisterhood through circlecraft, you cannot return to the too-small world. You are not the woman you once were; nor am I. You, like me, tried for a time to play by their rules and conform to their confining roles, but *no more*. No more do you hunch your shoulders and lower your eyes. No more do you pray quietly. No more do you go against what you know to be true, and no more do you fear the ways of the wise healer; She is you.

A certain and unfamiliar grief may overtake you now, my dear, and what you weep for is the loss of predictability. In the broom closet, you know where everything is; you know on which shelf you keep your childhood god, your sacred books, and your rituals. Once your spirituality has been unleashed in the wild world, you will no longer know precisely where each component of your practice rests, for it no longer rests at all. Your life as a Witch began long ago, Priestess, but opening that door, a door to which many women have been conditioned to turn their backs, will birth a newly integrated way of being; the process is akin to taking your first steps as a toddler. You are vibrant succulence reborn, and the grief you feel is for the loss of your simpler body-mind-only self. Stretch your wobbly legs and explore the wider world, but allow yourself to feel a good deal of confusion as well.

Given the chance, though, you would never irrevocably sacrifice your wide-awake, whole, integrated, and unapologetic movement through this perfect world of ours. You would not forever tether your wrists and toss away the keys that brought you out of the shadows. Your inner Witch knows there is no going back, and there can be no regression in the absence of your own agency; I am saying, my love, that if you choose to run back inside the broom closet and shut out the wild world, make sure it is you who is choosing. You are an autonomous woman who may well crave the solace of invisibility, but should you return to the shadows, know that your visit there will be short, for your liberation is permanent.

The Witch's Sacred Beliefs Inventory, Part I: Digging Up Dead Seeds

Take stock of what you believe now, Witch, and use this spiritual inventory as an affirmation of both your presence and your purpose. Light your candles, burn some dragon's blood resin, and raise your consciousness to the space between your soft animal brain and your bony skull; here, in this thin violet arc, vibrates the crown energy of higher consciousness. As you inhale, pull your spirit light down through your subtle and physical body. As you exhale, lift the crown energy up above you. You sit now in a protective egg of high-frequency divinity where your beliefs are easily accessed.

Begin to write now, my love, responding to this single prompt: "I believe that God-Goddess is…" You may need to repeat the prompt over and over again, but eventually you will strike at the heart of your beliefs regarding divinity. Find that core belief and mark it with holy pentagrams and joyful tears. Now ask yourself what lies beneath that core belief; where was that strong belief about divinity born? What is the parent belief undergirding it? Again, write, "I believe…" This time you are digging deep into the fertile soil of soul. Know that dark and apparently contradictory beliefs may emerge, and keep going. When you feel you have reached a pivotal belief, mark it again with sacred symbols. Go even deeper, and harvest what lies under this, and then under that, until you have unearthed beliefs so deeply seated that you scarcely recognize them as your own.

Perhaps indoctrinated ideas about religiosity emerge, planted in your little girl's psyche when she was too young to argue. You will likely uncover fears of abandonment and even death. Know that bringing these long-buried beliefs into the light of day is an important step in validating your spiritual transformation, regardless of the form that transformation is taking at the moment. Belief inventories help you recognize outmoded understandings that are not actually yours and therefore have no business informing your spiritual evolution. Any beliefs you uncover that feel wrong are consuming valuable resources that could be put to better use, and purging these dead seeds is an act of space creation.

The Witch's Sacred Beliefs Inventory, Part II: Turning the Fertile Ground Ritual

Gather your burning bowl, sage, fire maker, parchment, and pen; now meet me in the woods, my Sister. On one piece of parchment write all the dead-seed beliefs you are ready to purge. On another piece write all the beliefs you already harbor that are serving you well, amid others that feel very right but did not come up during the inventory exercise. These might include any of the following, but be sure any you use ring true in your bones: "I believe that a Witch is a wise, wild woman. I believe that a Witch is a compassionate healer of self, soul, and spirit, for herself as well as for the collective. I believe that the divine feminine will bring balance to the global community, and I believe I have a part in that awakening. I believe in the sanctity of my rituals and my magick. I believe in the value and nourishment of sisterhood. I believe every woman embodies every Goddess who has ever been revered and condemned, and every man embodies every god who has ever been revered and condemned. Separate, we are sacred masculine and feminine. Together, we are change agents for our wounded world. I believe that the

Earth is sacred, and I believe that all human souls are equally sanctified blood cells pulsing within the beating heart of the cosmos."

I am with you, Sister, when you read aloud the beliefs that no longer serve you and then set them afire. I am still with you when you toss dried sage leaves into the flames and feel your psychic landscape open and become brighter, surrendering to the aftermath of the wild blaze that cleared the fields. I am with you when you read your new beliefs, vows to the sacred self, and I am at your side getting dirt under my own nails when you bury the new beliefs in Gaia's fertile ground. Plant deeply these pranic seeds of fertile spirituality, and then nourish them with the practices that also feed your Witch's hungry belly.

FEEDING THE SHE-WOLF
She Does as She Wilt

As human beings, we have an ego-deep desire to label, fragment, and position concepts in opposition to one another. If it is not light, we label it as dark. If it is not marked by the attributes of the sacred feminine, we call it masculine. I hold a firm personal belief that the sacred feminine, when fed, will bring balance to an overly masculine world. However, I also recognize the sanctity of the divine masculine, it all its virile hunter and consciousness-raising glory, as well as the spectrum of wild spirituality on which everything I have spoken to you about in these pages lives.

When you feed the She-Wolf, you acknowledge that the defining trait of any wild spirituality is its resistance to limitations. The wild woman will be neither tamed nor labeled, for she is the embodiment of a billion concepts, deities, and holy energies at once. By extension, she will not go freely into space that is carved out for her; her priority is always liberation, which she achieves through a consistent and sensual experience of magick and Mystery. The She-Wolf wants to roam freely and in solitude at will. She wants to seek and find her pack when she needs them or when they howl for her. She will not be contained in any cage, even one you have built for her with your own hands.

She craves the raw meat of community and the rough sustenance of solitude in unpredictable waves of appetite, often needing one over the other for long periods. Just when you think you have her figured out, she will show you the deeper wild, a wild of the shadow-self for which you may feel ill prepared. Have faith in the arduous and organic process of your spiritual evolution, and trust that your She-Wolf knows exactly what She needs at every moment. You may not have a manual for her ways, and there is no tried-and-true process for appeasing the spiritually alive woman.

Resist the human temptation to fit each thing into its own beribboned box, and simply *be*. Be true to your nature. Be vibrant. Be authentic. Be you. Be wild. Listen to your Witch's voice growl and howl. See with the deep blue knowing of your third eye, and move into and through rather than *at* or against. The world needs your perfect presence and pure, feminine power, so I call on you to give full permission right now, in this moment, for your She-Magick to emanate out from your soft center at all times, from here to eternity.

Verses of the Holy Feminine
A Sinner's Morning Prayer

Bless my bare-breasted soul, for I will no longer call myself a sinner. No more will I forego my wildness or resist my temptation to be unapologetically free. Mother, I come to your table seeking abundance and grace, and I will wander the path of renunciation no more. I am answering your call, the call of the Holy Wild, and I will relish this world with all my senses.

Mother, I am untamed, and I have opened my legs to the moonlight. I have licked the sweet moss and painted my thighs with soft mud. I have ministered the marriage of my sex and spirit, and I consummate this

*union now with every breath I take. I have come home
to you, the one they tried to make me forget, and your
prodigal daughter will never lose her way again. I am
stripped bare of my good-girl nature, and there is no rigidity left in my bones.*

*As the bloody sun rises, for all these gifts I am about
to receive, accept my impassioned gratitude. This is the
morning prayer of the wild woman. May I feel the dirt
between my toes. May I bow deeply to the beauty of the
shadows, and may I take pause at moonrise to honor
all those in my matrilineal bloodline. So mote it be for
all women with whom I stand, so mote it be for me. All
blessings.*

FIERCE FORESIGHT
The Future of the Wild Woman

If we truly are birthing a sacred community of liberated spirituality,
marked as much by sensuality and creativity as by divinity, then, we
may ask, to what end do we do this? Is it a perfect utopia of holy healers
that will govern in circles, infusing the initiated and awakened masculine and feminine into all decisions? Will the daughters of our great-
granddaughters be told of their Goddess nature before they can walk?
Will our Earth be made whole before it is too late? What cosmic eruption will illuminate our skies to show us that we are being heard, that
we are headed in the right direction, and that all we are hoping for is
truly coming to us? I do not pretend to know the answer to these questions, my Sister, but I will tell you what I have seen in my lucid dreams
when my body is still and the room is dark.

I have seen a worldwide reclamation of the holy feminine that begins in parts of the world where women have achieved a certain level of
political, social, and economic autonomy that permits the liberation of
the sensual, creative, and spiritual wild; this is hardly an unchallenged

uprising, mind you, and it began decades ago with loud voices, strong conviction, and brave collective action. I have seen this movement erupting and spreading like wildfire, the flames fanned by women hearing, seeing, and feeling other women. I have seen men who embody the awakened, wild masculine standing strong and against other men who fear the loss of long-held power.

I have seen a great merging of spiritual traditions that sources a global integration of divine masculine and feminine in which no one is wrong, no one is doomed, and no one is cast out. I have seen the sun setting on a world where religiosity trumps spirituality, men rule over women, and all things, including gender, are defined and categorized to suit the powers that be. I have seen a great revolution led by visionaries and fueled by social media, and I have seen an emerging transparency where no one can hide behind closed doors.

I have seen all this, and I have seen your face there. Sister, I saw you standing with your fist raised in solidarity when the last woman was untied. I saw you weep when she finally danced, and I saw you hold her in a warm, maternal embrace. I saw little girls painting their faces with mud, and I saw little boys planting the spiritual seeds of the fertile wild. I saw still more children rejecting gender altogether, for they know the pulse of the masculine and feminine beats within us all, regardless of our biology. I have seen the full moon shining on your face, and I have seen you cast the circle that will manifest this world. I have seen you doing your sacred work, infusing magick into the most mundane of tasks, and I have seen you pass the talking stick to your sisters. Woman, I have seen you, and I call you a Woman Most Wild because I know who you are. You are she who cannot, who will not, be contained. You are she who is at home only when she has been liberated. You are limitless infinite. You are the bright light of spirit and the thick heat of soul. You are everything, wild woman. You are everything. You are everything. You are everything.

Epilogue

$\mathcal{W}$ild woman spirituality is precisely that; it is wild. It shifts and falls silent, shifts again and wails like gale-force winds, then, just when you think you have the patterns figured out and your path is perfectly paved, the ground quakes underneath you and sends all you know heaving and crashing to the mother-loving ground. Give permission to let your spiritual growth ebb and flow like the tide; there will be times when you are positively consumed by the magick and Mystery, when your intuitive third eye seems to see it all, and there will be times when you again trust nothing you cannot see with your first two eyes. The way of the wild woman takes *all* kinds, for she is all kinds. Let your spirituality be the stuff of alchemy. Let it wax, wane, and become the void, then see just as much mystic glamour in the nothingness as you do in the fullness. Knowing this, my love, truly *knowing* this, turn the third and final key.

My chin is quivering with anxious anticipation, and I am watching you with wet eyes. My mascara is running down my face like Witch's war paint, and I know, Sister, I *know* from the depths of my darkest places, that you are ready for this. Turn the key. Open the door. We are waiting for you with flower crowns and blessed water. Open the door, and come home to your wild self. Open the door, and reclaim the Witch as the wise healer who embodies the fierce feminine. Open the door, and liberate the Woman Most Wild.

Do this, and affirm the Witch as a wild woman of untamed honor and sensual, generative authenticity. Do this, and reclaim the name Witch as your own. Do this, and free yourself to be fiercely in and of the world, wielding and re-wilding the power of the feminine within your body and soul. Do this, and meet me where I stand. I want, my love, I want *so much* for you to stake your claim on what is yours. I want you to know that there is no tried-and-true formula for being a Witch, and there is no test to pass before you can say you have made it. I am telling you that the goallessness of the wild woman's spiral journey is where its perfection lies; you have already *made it*. Here we are, and so far we have come! Open the door, but do not do it just for you. Do it for the whole of our wild world, for it needs your magick desperately. So mote it be.

Verses of the Holy Feminine
The Soul Marriage

The Bride stood in front of the ancient mirror, raised her red hood, struck a match, and lit the garnet-bejeweled candle. "I am here," she whispered, now lighting the violet candle, her reflection illumined by the flames of soul and spirit as much as by the milky moonlight. "I am here." She licked her lips, readying herself for the most important vows she would ever take, and held the unlit emerald-green candle between both shaking hands. Her gaze met her own wet eyes in the mirror, and she began:

"*Dearly beloved, I am here to marry my own sacred self underneath these Tantric stars. I am here to bind my venerable sexuality and majestic feminine roots to my undying divinity, and tonight I forge the enduring connection between my soul and spirit out of blood, bone, and my holy heart.*"

A warm, too-strong breeze let the Bride know the Mystery was listening, and she continued. "*I vow to honor my body's connection to its wild nature wholly and often, to feel the ecstatic pulse of new birth in spring, orgasmic fruition in summer, nature's death rattle in autumn, and the fertile darkness of winter. I vow to give myself permission to feel it all, to change in every way, every day, if I must, and to hug close the other members of the She-Kingdom of Nature.*"

The trees bent back now in the Bride's honor, and she was heartened. She took her red hood down and bellowed the next vows moonward with a guttural growl: "*I vow to not think my body is any less than perfection, and nor will I let anyone else try to claim it as their own. This blood and these bones are mine and mine alone. I vow I will not stand down when my sisters cannot stand up.*

"*I vow I will pray with my whole body, and belly dance with my spirit at the time of my death. No longer will anyone cage my spirituality.*"

The Bride nestled the still-unlit green candle in the dirt before the mirror and continued: "*I vow I will not think myself anything less than pure divinity, for I am a She-God. This body is a flawless temple to Her, and the Church of the Holy Wild knows no rules written by the hands of the oppressors.*"

She took the red candle of soul in her right hand and the violet spirit candle in her left. "*I am the Bride of Eternal Mystery, and I do hereby take my soul to love,* honor, and cherish in darkness and in light, in this life and on into the next."

The Bride lit the heart candle now with the dual flames of soul and spirit, tilting her head back in ecstasy and feeling all three flames warm and lick away the walls she had built between her sensual, sexual self and her impeccable divine nature. She cried out to the darkness now: "By the power vested in me by the Ministry of the Unruined, I now pronounce myself a Woman Most Wild."

The Bride put her flat, still-quivering palm on her tear-streaked reflection, nodding sharply in solidarity with the woman she once was, now is, and will forever be. "All blessings be," she whispered. "By the grace of all hallowed things, all blessings be."

Appendix

Moon Rituals for Lone Wolf-Women and Witches' Circles

Remember that the best Book of Shadows is the one written in your own hand, and the spirituality of the wild woman must be fiercely, personally relevant. The following topics and rituals are suggestions only, and every Witch should openly explore the practices that speak most loudly to her soul at any given moment. Do not feel bound by supposed-tos or should-bes. Know that this Craft is yours and yours alone, and your growth depends on the integration of your unique soul with your universally connected spirit.

WINTER'S MOONS

Approximate dates in the Northern Hemisphere: December 21–March 20
Approximate dates in the Southern Hemisphere: June 21–September 20
Goddess phases: Crone in early winter; Maiden in late winter
Chakral correspondences: Third eye and crown in early winter; root in late winter

Elemental correspondences: Air and ether in early winter; Earth in late winter

Directional correspondences: Northwest in early winter; northeast in late winter

The Long Night's Moon

ENERGIES

Reverence, rest, ritual

FOR LONE WOLF-WOMEN: A SELFISH FEAST

My Sister, it will be difficult, but carve out a bit of space-time for yourself as the Long Night's Moon waxes, and set a table for one. Prepare a balanced but hearty meal of fresh, unprocessed foods. Light your candles and smell the evergreens, for you are safe, warm, and fed. Afford attention to every single burst of flavor in your mouth. Chew slowly. Honor the miraculous journey the food has taken from farm to table. Consider the immense amount of energy that has been invested in bringing this meal to your mouth, and revel in sheer gratitude every time you swallow. Witch, affirm your fearlessness and divine right to sustenance, for you are a woman safe in your winter nest.

FOR THE WITCHES' CIRCLE: AUTHENTIC GIFT GIVING
AND HOLY HANDIWORK

The moon of the winter solstice honors the return of the solar light. The moon is holding space for the sun during the autumn months when the solar energy is low, and this Long Night's Moon acknowledges that this burden is being lifted. Show appreciation for one another at this time, and offer gifts to your wild sisters. Honor your circle as holy, and bless the coming year with your communion.

The Wolf Moon

ENERGIES

Intuition, solitude, roving in darkness

For Lone Wolf-Women: A Meditation for Meeting the Midwinter Crone

Find yourself on the edge of a deep winter's sleep now, Priestess of the Ice-Pond. Call to mind this scene: You stand at the edge of a frozen body of water, the full Wolf Moon barely showing behind thick, gray clouds. A layer of frost covers the ground, and your breath fogs in a steady beat of exhales. A single wolf's howl hearkens the arrival of the hooded Crone, moving toward you slowly and without effort across the frozen lake. Her lined face tells you She is wise, and this Soul Mother has something to tell you. What does this grandmother tell you of winter? What tasks has She for your soul's deep nourishment?

For Witches' Circles: Divination Magick

Often the first moon of the solar year, the energies of the Wolf Moon may call the circle to engage in discussions and exercises that cultivate women's intuition. This moon is infused with receptive energy; it is a lunar cycle of sensory exploration rather than active manifestation. Honor the Wolf Moon through oracle, wild divination, meditation, and dream-work, permitting all members of the circle to engage their diamond-light third eyes and practice psychic skills.

The Quickening Moon

Energies

New life, stirring in the shadows, fierce vigilance

For Lone Wolf-Women: Seed Blessing

Under the Quickening Moon, channel the high-fire energy by charging wildflower seeds; cup the seeds in your hands and honor their energetic potential for life. Feel the Quickening of life inside the seeds as mirroring that inside your root chakra, and let all of this life-giving prana feed the seeds now. Attune to the seeds' energy and see if they begin to feel full, as if the energetic capacity has been reached. Now plant these seeds and charge them a bit more every day, until the Quickening Moon has completed its cycle.

For Witches' Circles: Rebirth and Ritual

Quickening Moon energy can feel manic and overwhelming both on an individual level and for the circle as a whole. Acknowledge the nature of this lunar energy, and afford all women the opportunity to voice their experiences with this energy in their everyday lives. This moon generally falls in the weeks following Imbolc, a solar Sabbat or holiday during which the vital and fertile essence of the coming spring is acknowledged. Channel the Quickening Moon energy into a ritual or spell that acknowledges the pranic spark of new birth; this can be seed planting, nest building, or any creative ceremony that allows circle members to embed this midwinter energy into an early act of manifestation.

Spring's Moons

Approximate dates in the Northern Hemisphere: March 21–June 20
Approximate dates in the Southern Hemisphere: September 21–December 20
Goddess phase: Maiden
Chakral correspondences: Root in early spring; sacral in late spring
Elemental correspondences: Earth in early spring; water in late spring
Directional correspondence: East

The Storm Moon

Energies

Sensuality, surrender

For Lone Wolf-Women: Surrendering to the Fury

Have no expectations, for the storm writhes inside you with all the frantic intentions of a mother bird building her nest. The Storm Moon holds a furious energy, but you sense that the frenzy is temporary. You may also have a deep understanding that fighting the storm with plans and purpose is absolutely futile. Close your eyes, my love, and let the droplets beat your bare breasts. This is not the end, but the perfect work of labor. Let the storm threaten your old life, and unleash the birth-waters of the new. Surrender to the fury, and know that you were born for just this. Ask yourself what needs to manifest now, by the light of the Storm Moon.

For Witches' Circles: The Wild Creative

Arriving around the vernal equinox, the Storm Moon is a sudden eruption of the swirling high-fire energies building since the winter solstice. Circle-craft at this time of year can begin active manifestation undergirded with an intent to surrender to the Storm; an element of not-knowing walks along with purposeful action at this time, and painting, creating spell bags, shaping some clay, and other such works in which each circle member becomes the Creatrix Herself, even for a short time within the sacred circle, fosters opportunities for women to affirm their fem-force when the lunar energies are so fierce that women can feel disempowered.

The Hawk Moon

Energies

Divination, foresight

For Lone Wolf-Women: The Witch's Gift from the Sea

An intimate connection exists, psychic Sister, between your third-eye chakra, your fertile center of intuition, and your sacral center; this connection is amplified under the Hawk Moon, with your inner Maiden squinting to see in the dim light as the storm passes. Call to mind this image: You are standing on a rain-soaked beach under darkened skies, but the celestial rumbles are growing softer in the distance. Look out onto the deep blue ocean as it calms, low waves rising and falling on the shore. Dig your toes into the cold wet sand and raise your arms high. Beckon the sea to bring you a token of your desire now. Let a wave carry this symbol of what the remaining months of spring hold for you. What do you find there on the shore? Hold it in your hands and touch it to your third eye, then to womb-center. Offer gratitude to the water nymphs and sea faeries for granting you the gift of foresight as the storm passes. All is coming.

FOR WITCHES' CIRCLES: STAR-SCRYING

The time to engage in fierce foresight is here, under the Hawk Moon. Let your Witches' Circle focus on wild divination scrying. If you have a clear night, let your circle meet under the moon. Have everyone bring blankets and pillows, and ask them to call to mind a particular question about the coming lunar cycle before looking to the stars. What do you see there? Does your answer come from a twinkling constellation or a bright, constant planet promising steadfastness? Do you see a shooting meteorite, promising good fortune? Find your answers in the night sky with your sisters.

The Budding Trees' Moon

ENERGIES

Growth, trust, manifestation

FOR LONE WOLF-WOMEN: JUMPING THE BROOM

Creatrix-Witch, fashion your broom from a large branch and twigs, tying silky ribbons to hold the small twig-bristles in place. You will not be using this to sweep, Hearth-Holder, so pay no mind to the cleaning functionality of your magickal tool. This broom is a gateway to the next great step on your soul path. Lay the broom horizontal in front of a full-length mirror, then back away! From a distance, begin to run fast and run hard toward your summer dreams. Your track is akin to your future's birth canal; all that is behind you, all that is your past, will die when you take the leap. Now jump, Priestess! Stand in front of the mirror and proclaim your rebirth!

FOR WITCHES' CIRCLES: BUDDING TREES' COUNCIL

The Moon of Budding Trees heralds a time of intense manifestation. Circle-crafting as midspring approaches should empower members to acknowledge the merit of their dreams, their agency in creating the life they desire, and, very important, the role of the circle in objectively framing those *wants* into transformative alchemy. Council work at this time is powerful and invaluable; it allows women to bring their life visions for sacred work, home, relationship, health, spiritual integrity, and other components of a life well nourished out of their heads and into a lower, more manifested vibration. The circle may choose to combine council with spellcraft or creative work, all the while ensuring that communication is authentic and feminine.

SUMMER'S MOONS

Approximate dates in the Northern Hemisphere: June 21–September 20
Approximate dates in the Southern Hemisphere: December 21–March 20
Goddess phase: Mother
Chakral correspondences: Solar plexus, heart, and throat
Elemental correspondences: Fire and air
Directional correspondence: South

The Strong Sun Moon

ENERGIES
Fullness, enjoyment, wild abandon

FOR LONE WOLF-WOMEN: AN ACT OF HEDONISM

Find yourself at midnight on the shortest eve of Midsummer, and shed your skin of propriety. Run like the untamed wolf you are, and do things your day-self would call forbidden. There is nothing but you and the moon now, wild Witch, and no one will see you if you lick a tree or pleasure yourself in a cool stream. Your lust on this magick night is for your own body, and no lover could ever be as fitting. Dig your hands into the mud, my love, and paint your face with Gaia's blood. Act as a newly uncaged animal, for no one is stopping you. Break all the patterns with which you have been indoctrinated, for tonight you are a beauteous beast.

FOR WITCHES' CIRCLES: NATURE'S SOUL-RETRIEVAL

At no other time of year is the marriage between the sun and moon more apparent than around the summer solstice. The sacred masculine and sacred feminine are revered at this time, and it may feel right to welcome into the circle those with strong, masculine energy, including men. The Strong Sun Moon is ripe for supporting environmental consciousness. The circle may feel called to retrieve pieces of Mother Nature's soul, a shamanic ceremony that can be incredibly powerful when done in circle.

The Blessing Moon

ENERGIES
    Gratitude, abundance

FOR LONE WOLF-WOMEN: THE ALTAR OF THE GRATEFUL WITCH

Build an Altar of the Grateful Witch, decorating this sacred place with representations of all you hold dear. Photographs of loved ones, members of your found family and blood family, and mystical places you have been or wish to go are interspaced with fruit, flowers, and natural tokens of Gaia's royalty. Have all you most truly value reflected here, my love, and let these things expand for you as the Blessing Moon waxes toward fullness. Light candles here, and know no scarcity, for you are a Witch whose trust fund is full of moonbeams and faeries' wings. All blessings be!

FOR WITCHES' CIRCLES: GRATITUDE CHANT AND WAND BLESSING

Blessing Moon energy is fertile, and circle-craft grounded in gratitude can be very transformative at this time. Women's expressions of gratitude for abundance in their lives create critical ripples in the cosmic fabric. Base spellwork, ritual, and discussions of the Blessing Moon on offering gratitude for the present moment rather than manifesting for future or healing the past.

The Corn Moon

ENERGIES
    Reaping, culmination

FOR LONE WOLF-WOMEN: HARVESTING THE SHADOW-SELF

With summer's looming end comes an inner knowing of the shadow's emergence. Your belly fire may seek to cling to what it knows to be familiar and safe, but, my love, do not let it; once you know for sure that a part of your identity is no longer authentic, rid yourself of this baggage. Dig your shovel deep into the summer ground now, Goddess of the Harvest, for underneath the dirt lies a part of you purposefully suppressed. Dig deep and dig hard, now. Let sweat bead on your forehead and soak your clothes, for shadow work is a dark labor of soul. Ask yourself what parts of your identity have been long buried but now need to surface. Ask yourself what you disdain about others and, there, find your own suppressed truths. Do you reject those who play the victim? Perhaps you long for vulnerability. Do you scorn those women who show too much skin? Perhaps you long to show your own nakedness to the world. Dig up your shadow, Witch, for it will serve you well when the void of autumn calls you home.

FOR WITCHES' CIRCLES: HESTIA'S BREW CIRCLE
AND COMMUNAL DINNER

As autumn approaches, the turning of the wheel can foster strong feelings of independence, loneliness, and unexplainable grief in women who are experiencing the collective and cyclical end to nature's fertility and abundance. The moons of autumn all begin to steadily reflect the veil's permeability, and circle-craft at this time can honor the pending fallow times through nourishment of the physical body. Cook together. Eat together. Give a nod to your root chakras, and prepare yourself for the coming harvest.

AUTUMN'S MOONS

Approximate dates in the Northern Hemisphere: September 21–
December 20
Approximate dates in the Southern Hemisphere: March 21–June 20
Goddess phases: Mother in early autumn; Crone in late autumn
Chakral correspondences: Third eye and crown

Elemental correspondences: Air and ether
Directional correspondence: West

The Harvest Moon

ENERGIES
Change, independence, transformation

FOR LONE WOLF-WOMEN: A HEART-LIGHT LETTER

Human beings are empathic by nature, though we have learned to guard against feeling our connection to others too deeply. The Harvest Moon initiates a path of rebirth for your inner Witch and, by the light of this moon, you must acknowledge your most challenging teachers. Take up your pen, Witch, and write a letter of deep forgiveness to someone who has wronged you. Know that forgiveness does not mean condoning their actions; it is an act of liberation through which you become free of attachment to their part in your story. Begin the letter by telling them precisely how they made you feel, and do not edit yourself. Every emotion is valid. Now begin to acknowledge what it must have been like to be in their proverbial shoes. Remember that given what they know, what they had been taught, and all other deep patterns, they were acting as they thought best at the time. Now, my love, end with words of forgiveness and compassion: *I forgive you to free myself, and I acknowledge our shared part in the human story.* By the light of the Harvest Moon, burn this letter with a bit of sage, and inhale the scent of severed ties and freedom.

FOR WITCHES' CIRCLES: SURRENDER AND FIRE-PURGE RITUAL

The Harvest Moon is powerful, and if possible, grounding circle-craft in surrender and letting go is ideal at this time. Purge with fire all that does not belong in each other's lives any longer, and engage in banishing spells if necessary. This is the time of the wealthy feminine, my love, and your circle will mutually support itself in removing obstacles to its liberation.

The Blood Moon

ENERGIES

Conclusion, death, mourning

FOR LONE WOLF-WOMEN: THE WITCH'S BATTLEFIELD

Call attention to your throat chakra and know it as the center of your voice, truth, and story. Envision yourself on a muddy field following a fierce and epic battle. Among the dying lies your younger self, and you cradle her in your arms. Hold her and whisper words of loving support to ease the transition; these are the words you need to hear most right now as you enter the void of late autumn and the nights grow long and cold. Say aloud the words you would say to your younger self as she falls away into the realm of Spirit. What does she need to hear as the light dims in her eyes? This is your battlefield, Witch, and you have emerged victorious. The casualty is your past, for you are no longer this woman who lies dying in your arms. Whisper words of grief and honor, then let her pass.

FOR WITCHES' CIRCLES: ANCESTOR HONORING AND THE DUMB SUPPER

The veil is at its thinnest around the Blood Moon. Use this time for honoring your ancestors in circle with a Dumb Supper ritual. A traditional Dumb Supper is consumed in solemn silence in memory of those who have passed. You may choose to bring a particular ancestor as guest, cook her or his favorite food, and invite this being to sit with you in circle. This can be a powerfully healing ritual if you bring a female ancestor whom you know could have benefited from a Witches' Circle like yours.

The Ancestors Moon

ENERGIES

Remembrance, honor, reverence

For Lone Wolf-Women: Seeing Spirit without Fear

Your third eye can see much that your conscious mind does not register. Because the subtle energies that surround us are not as threatening to our physical safety as that which is material and heavy, our primal brain deems these energies unimportant. Mind you, this world is no less real than our denser surroundings, and, my Spirit-Sister, you have nothing to fear. Shield yourself in this way first, my love: Envision your aura running through you and surrounding you in an egg of white light. On the outer edge of this energetic shell is a crystalline layer that is impermeable from the outside. Nothing can come in, and you are safe. Now go to a wild place when the moon is high and the night is long, or go to your wild sanctuary within your home. Sit in silence and look into the night. Are there vibrating foggy energies in this place? Are there orbs moving with purpose? See those in the ether without labeling them, for these beings do not like to be contained by such names. Witch, your third eye is open. Use your vision well.

For Witches' Circles: Serenity in the Mystery Spell

The moons between Samhain and the winter solstice are high-frequency moons with raw spiritual vibrations. It is best for circle-craft at this time to tune in to the needs of the circle; it may feel appropriate to honor the uneasy perfection of not-knowing and Mystery. Be kind to one another at this time of year, and know that deep transformations are likely occurring under the surface of the women's lives.

The Thirteenth Moon

Energies

The holy void, sacred mystery

For Lone Wolf-Women: Building a Nest

Carve out two hours for yourself under the Thirteenth Moon; schedule this time as if it were for a critical, unmissable meeting, as pressing as any familial obligation. Now build yourself a soft, healing nest of pillows and blankets. Surround yourself with dripping red candles and play soft, instrumental music. Be a Goddess on the Nest now, just for this time. Affirm that you have nowhere else to go and nothing that needs immediate doing. You are here. You are safe. You are home.

For Witches' Circles: Council for Feminine Healing

Councils held just before the winter solstice are ideal for support and feminine healing. It seems every woman is losing something, giving some great part of her life up in order to make room for something better. Hold space for one another to grieve. Engage in spellcraft or ritual as feels appropriate, but force nothing. There is bliss in the darkness now. Blessed be the longest night. Blessed be the light. Blessed be the dark. All blessings be.

Acknowledgments

This book would not have been possible had my own inner Witch not been liberated so many years ago. It was through the loving counsel of many friends, family members, fellow writers, and mentors that She was freed from the limiting beliefs of a rigidly religious childhood. I would like to thank my sons, Bodhi and Sage, for their acceptance of their Mama's wild spiritual path, my partner, Ryan, for his tender support and continual reflection of the Sacred Masculine embodied in a bearded, guitar-strumming potter, and my grandmother, Grace, for her selfless love when she was alive and her messages of enduring encouragement from the realm of Spirit.

Thank you to my council of five women for helping me streamline the vision for my sacred work and make the birth of this book possible. To Susan for creating and holding the studio space where my soul-work is housed so warmly, to all the men and women who have graduated from the Living Mandala Yoga teacher training programs over the years, and to the entire community of Phoenixville, Pennsylvania, I bow down to you in fierce gratitude for your weird, eclectic wisdoms, wide-open hearts, and unconditional love.

I would like to thank my literary agent, Sheree Bykofsky; my editor, Georgia Hughes; and everyone from New World Library for making publication possible and spreading the wild word. To all my online readers who send messages of understanding and gratitude and who share their stories with me, your words have continually validated my work and given me the courage to write this book. I will keep howling for you, as the wild feminine will keep howling through me.

Finally, to whatever ethereal decision led to my soul's mandate in this life, I say thank you. If there is an Ascended Master who gave me a nod, if I committed some great karmic act in a previous life that warranted reward, or if there was some spiraling, cosmic chaos that somehow solidified into this life of mine and allowed the Holy Feminine to speak through me, know I am forever grateful.

Notes

Introduction

Page 3   *It was not so long ago*: See Anne Llewellyn Barstow, *Witchcraze: A New History of the European Witch Hunts* (San Francisco: HarperCollins, 1994), for an account of historic and modern Witch-hunts as a tool of oppression.

Page 4   Coven *is a very broad term*: See Amber K, *Covencraft: Witchcraft for Three or More* (Woodbury, MN: Llewellyn, 1998), for a Wiccan perspective on coven history and evolution.

Page 6   *All human beings*: See Anodea Judith, *The Global Heart Awakens: Humanity's Rite of Passage from the Love of Power to the Power of Love* (San Rafael, CA: Shift Books, 2013), for a discussion of human history from a masculine and feminine perspective.

Chapter 1. The Holy Moon and Your Witch Consciousness

Page 15   *The philosophy of Tantra teaches us*: See Sally Kempton, *Awakening Shakti: The Transformative Power of the Goddesses of Yoga* (Boulder, CO: Sounds True, 2013), for a discussion of Tantra from a feminine perspective.

Page 16   *Your Witch consciousness*: See Demetra George, *Mysteries of the Dark*

Moon: The Healing Power of the Dark Goddess (San Francisco: HarperCollins, 1992), for a discussion of lunar phases and their impact on the psyche.

Page 18   *Clarissa Pinkola Estés, in her treatise*: Clarissa Pinkola Estés, *Women Who Run with the Wolves* (New York: Ballantine, 1992), 277.

Page 22   *If we are always unlearning limiting beliefs*: See Bill Plotkin, *Soulcraft: Crossing into the Mysteries of Nature and Psyche* (Novato, CA: New World Library, 2003), for an in-depth examination of soul as separate from, though intimately related to, ego and spirit.

Page 25   *The womb-wounds of women*: See Padma Aon Prakasha and Anaiya Aon Prakasha, *Womb Wisdom: Awakening the Creative and Forgotten Powers of the Feminine* (Rochester: Destiny Books, 2011), for womb-clearing practices and meditations.

Page 26   *Women who share their sexual stories*: See Jalaja Bonheim, *Aphrodite's Daughters: Women's Sexual Stories and the Journey of the Soul* (New York: Touchstone, 1997), for a brilliant compilation of women's sexual stories.

Page 27   *In* What We Ache For: Oriah Mountain Dreamer, *What We Ache For: Creativity and the Unfolding of Your Soul* (San Francisco: HarperCollins, 2005), 201.

Page 30   *Anodea Judith defines empathy*: Judith, *Global Heart Awakens*, 133.

Page 31   *The levels of grief*: See Elisabeth Kübler-Ross and David Kessler, *On Grief and Grieving: Finding the Meaning of Grief through the Five Stages of Loss* (New York: Scribner, 2005), for an in-depth theoretical discussion of the five stages of grief.

CHAPTER 2. THE RIGHTEOUS SUN AND YOUR PRIESTESS'S FIRE

Page 39   *Bill Plotkin writes in* Soulcraft: Bill Plotkin, *Soulcraft: Crossing into the Mysteries of Nature and Psyche* (Novato, CA: New World Library, 2003), 332.

Page 43   *In* Goddesses in Everywoman: Jean Shinoda Bolen, *Goddesses in Every Woman: A New Psychology of Women* (New York: HarperPerennial, 1984), 283.

Page 46   *These are the moments when*: See Anodea Judith and Lion Goodman, *Creating on Purpose: The Spiritual Technology of Manifesting through the Chakras* (Boulder, CO: Sounds True, 2012), 86–87. Judith and Goodman discuss how to track your life's purpose by outlining moments in your path when you felt most *you*.

Page 47   *Personal mythwork is an invaluable tool*: See Plotkin, *Soulcraft*, 205, for more on personal mythwork.

Page 52   *Living in rhythm with the sun and moon*: See Andre Van Lysebeth, *Tantra: The Cult of the Feminine* (Boston, MA: Weiser Books, 1995), for a philosophical and historical study of Tantra.

Chapter 3. The Wild Feminine and Your Blood Rhythms

Page 54   *In* Sophia: Goddess of Wisdom: Caitlín Matthews, *Sophia: Goddess of Wisdom, Bride of God* (Wheaton, IL: Quest Books, 2001).

Page 54   *The loss of the spiritual self*: See Bill Plotkin, *Wild Mind: A Field Guide to the Human Psyche* (Novato, CA: New World Library, 2013), 199–202. Plotkin highlights addiction and escape from a spiritual perspective.

Page 55   *Her blood is fearsome*: See Demetra George, *Mysteries of the Dark Moon: The Healing Power of the Dark Goddess* (San Francisco: HarperCollins, 1992), 6–22.

Page 57   *Judith Duerk writes*: Judith Duerk, *Circle of Stones: Woman's Journey to Herself* (Novato, CA: New World Library, 2004), 70.

Chapter 4. Hallowed Yoga and Your Energy Alchemy

Page 66   *Yoga, in its most authentic and practical definition*: The Yoga Sutras of Patanjali, 1.1.

Page 66   *Spirit is why you are here*: See Bill Plotkin, *Soulcraft* (Novato, CA: New World Library, 2003), for information on distinguishing soul from spirit.

Page 67   *Inside your lower three chakras*: See Anodea Judith, *Eastern Body, Western Mind: Psychology and the Chakra System as a Path to the Self* (Berkeley, CA: Celestial Arts, 1996), for an in-depth exploration of the chakral system from the dual perspectives of Eastern philosophy and Western psychology.

Page 71   *Yoga holds the power to remove*: Shiva Rea, *Tending the Heart-Fire: Living in Flow with the Pulse of Life* (Boulder, CO: Sounds True, 2014), 5.

Page 71   *Your root chakra is your oldest chakra*: See Judith, *Eastern Body, Western Mind*, 51–102, for more information on the root chakra.

Page 73   *At your sacral center*: See Judith, *Eastern Body, Western Mind*, 104–63, for more information on the sacral chakra.

Page 76   *Your Manipura chakra*: See Judith, *Eastern Body, Western Mind*, 167–219, for more information on the solar plexus chakra.

Page 78   *All the gifts your soul has designed*: See Judith, *Eastern Body, Western Mind*, 221–83, for more information on the heart chakra.

Page 78   *At your violet Spirit crown*: See Judith, *Eastern Body, Western Mind*, for more on the throat chakra, 285–335, third-eye chakra, 337–88, and crown chakra, 390–437.

Chapter 5: Circle-Casting and Your Wild Ecology

Page 90   *Each of the directions*: See Shiva Rea, *Tending the Heart-Fire* (Boulder, CO: Sounds True, 2014), 108–9, for an overview of *rasa*.

Page 91   *The northern aspects of the feminine*: See Bill Plotkin, *Wild Mind* (Novato, CA: New World Library, 2013), 33–50, for a discussion of the northern aspects of the human psyche.

Page 95   *The East is the direction*: See Plotkin, *Wild Mind*, 77–95, for a discussion of the eastern aspects of the human psyche.

Page 98   *The South is a volatile, passionate agent*: See Plotkin, *Wild Mind*, 51–75, for a discussion of the southern aspects of the human psyche.

Page 101   *The West is the direction of watery mystery*: See Plotkin, *Wild Mind*, 97–102, for a discussion of the western aspects of the human psyche.

CHAPTER 6. A PRIESTESS-HEALER'S SPELLWORK

Page 107   *In rebinding the Witch*: See *The Yoga Sutras of Patanjali* for the original discussion on yogic ethics and nonharming.

Page 108   *In The Global Heart Awakens*: Anodea Judith, *The Global Heart Awakens: Humanity's Rite of Passage from the Love of Power to the Power of Love* (San Rafael, CA: Shift Books, 2013), 183.

Page 110   *Before you surrender the spell*: See Serena Roney-Dougal, *Where Science and Magic Meet* (Somerset, UK: Green Magic, 2010), for an in-depth study on magick from a scientific perspective.

Page 110   *In yogic ethics*: See *Yoga Sutras* for the original discussion of *isvara pranidhana*.

Page 111   *Human beings have an intimate connection*: See Roney-Dougal, *Where Science and Magic Meet*, 140–46, for a scientific discussion on the human body's relationship to the Earth's electromagnetic field.

Page 118   *The whole of our economy*: See Lynne Twist, *The Soul of Money: Transforming Your Relationship with Money and Life* (New York: Norton, 2003). Twist discusses the global economy from a feminine perspective, emphasizing sufficiency over scarcity.

CHAPTER 7. THE WILD GODDESS MINISTRY

Page 127   *She often has to examine*: See Demetra George, *Mysteries of the Dark Moon: The Healing Power of the Dark Goddess* (San Francisco: HarperCollins, 1992), for a thorough account of the suppression of Goddess culture at various points of human civilization's growth.

Page 129   *Know that you need not name Her*: Caitlín Matthews, *Sophia: Goddess of Wisdom, Bride of God* (Wheaton, IL: Quest Books, 2001), 28.

Page 131   *Hold steadfast to this truth*: See Sally Kempton, *Awakening Shakti: The Transformative Power of the Goddesses of Yoga* (Boulder, CO: Sounds True, 2013), 11–23.

CHAPTER 8. PRAYERFUL PATHWORKING AND DEEP BEING

Page 133   *This traditional Pagan mythos*: See Ann Moura, *Grimoire for the Green Witch: A Complete Book of Shadows* (Woodbury, MN: Llewellyn, 2006), 10–11, for a Wiccan perspective on the Wheel of the Year and the relationship between God and Goddess.

Page 135   *LaSara Firefox writes*: LaSara Firefox, *Sexy Witch* (Woodbury, MN: Llewellyn, 2005), 3.

Page 138   *A woman is slowly separated*: See Serena Roney-Dougal, *Where Science and Magic Meet* (Green Magic, 2010), 89–127, for an articulation of psychic development during adolescence.

Page 141   *You are a child of nature*: See Kaleo Ching and Elise Dirlam Ching, *Faces of Your Soul: Rituals in Art, Maskmaking, and Guided Imagery with Ancestors, Spirit Guides, and Totem Animals* (Berkeley, CA: North Atlantic Books, 2006), for a wealth of animal totem and spirit guide meditations from a shamanic perspective.

Page 145   *Exploring the psychic realm*: Ching and Ching, *Faces of Your Soul*, 64–91.

CHAPTER 9. THE BLESSED MAGICK OF CIRCLE-CRAFT

Page 155   *No member of the circle*: See Jalaja Bonheim, *The Sacred Ego: Making Peace with Ourselves and Our World* (Berkeley, CA: North Atlantic Books, 2015). Bonheim discusses the role of the ego in women's circles.

Page 159   *Ascend the ego*: Bonheim, *Sacred Ego*, 5–29.

Page 161   *In* Circle of Stones: Judith Duerk, *Circle of Stones: Woman's Journey to Herself* (Novato, CA: New World Library, 2004), 99.

Page 164   *In* Women Who Run with the Wolves: Clarissa Pinkola Estés, *Women Who Run with the Wolves: Myths and Stories of the Wild Woman Archetype* (New York: Ballantine, 1992), 304.

CHAPTER 10. THE WITCH'S MEDICINE AND MIDWIFING THE CIRCLE

Page 167   *Circles are organically formed*: See Susanne Fincher, *The Mandala Workbook: A Creative Guide for Self-Exploration, Balance, and Well-Being* (Boston, MA: Shambhala, 2009), 1–21.

Page 172   *You may open the meeting*: See Robin Rose Bennett, *Healing Magic: A Green Witch Guidebook to Conscious Living* (New York: Sterling, 2004), for simple herbal correspondences and basic spell-casting information.

Page 172   *You, as the circle's creatrix*: See Jalaja Bonheim, *The Sacred Ego: Making*

Peace with Ourselves and Our World (Berkeley, CA: North Atlantic Books, 2015), for heart-based communication strategies.

CHAPTER 11. THE WILD COUNCIL AND PACK LIFE

Page 179   *There is no typical circle*: See Jean Shinoda Bolen, *The Millionth Circle: How to Change Ourselves and the World* (Berkeley, CA: Conari, 1999), for a discussion of the women's circle's role in effecting global change.

Page 181   *The ritual of the actual meeting*: See Bolen, *Millionth Circle*, for information on the circle's life cycle.

Page 183   *Here I want to note that*: See Bill Plotkin, *Soulcraft: Crossing into the Mysteries of Nature and Psyche* (Novato, CA: New World Library, 2003), 150–59. Plotkin discusses council work as a soul-based practice.

Page 186   *Do not discount the merit*: See Clarissa Pinkola Estés, *Women Who Run with the Wolves: Myths and Stories of the Wild Woman Archetype*, 177–212, for a discussion of belonging's merit for the wild woman.

CHAPTER 12. BENEDICTION OF THE LIBERATED WOLF-WOMAN

Page 189   *When the ego acknowledges*: Estés, *Women Who Run*, 38–39.

Page 191   *Take stock of what you believe now*: See Anodea Judith and Lion Goodman, *Creating on Purpose: The Spiritual Technology of Manifesting through the Chakras* (Boulder, CO: Sounds True, 2012), for various belief examination practices.

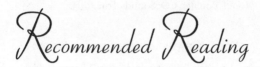

Recommended Reading

CREATIVE WORK AND PAINTING

Bowley, Flora. *Brave Intuitive Painting: Techniques for Uncovering Your Own Unique Painting Style*. Beverly, MA: Quarry Books, 2012.

Fincher, Susanne F. *Creating Mandalas: For Insight, Healing, and Self-Expression*. Boston, MA: Shambhala, 2010.

Kent, Tami Lynn. *Wild Creative: Igniting Your Passion and Potential in Home, Work, and Life*. New York: Atria Books, 2014.

Verdugo, Tracy. *Paint Mojo: A Mixed-Media Workshop*. Cincinnati: North Light Books, 2014.

MAGICK, RITUAL, AND CEREMONY

Conway, D. J. *Moon Magick: Myths & Magic, Crafts & Recipes, Rituals & Spells*. Woodbury, MN: Llewellyn, 2010.

Deerman, Dixie, and Steve Rasmussen. *The Goodly Spellbook: Olde Spells for Modern Problems*. New York: Sterling Ethos, 2014.

Farmer, Steven D. *Sacred Ceremony: How to Create Ceremonies for Healing, Transitions, and Celebrations*. Carlsbad, CA: Hay House, 2002.

Zell-Ravenheart, Morning Glory, and Oberon Zell-Ravenheart. *Creating Circles and Ceremonies*. Wayne, NJ: New Page Books, 2006.

FEMINIST SPIRITUALITY

Beak, Sera. *Red Hot and Holy: A Heretic's Love Story*. Boulder, CO: Sounds True, 2015.

Estés, Clarissa Pinkola. *Untie the Strong Woman: Blessed Mothers' Immaculate Love for the Wild Soul*. Boulder, CO: Sounds True, 2013.

YOGA, CHAKRAS, AND SUBTLE ENERGY

Feuerstein, Georg. *The Yoga Tradition: Its History, Literature, Philosophy, and Practice*. Prescott, AZ: Hohm Press, 2001.

Gawain, Shakti. *Creative Visualization: Use the Power of Your Imagination to Create What You Want in Your Life*. Novato, CA: New World Library, 2002.

Iyengar, B. K. S. *Light on Yoga: Yoga Dipika*. New York: Schocken, 1979.

Peirce, Penney. *Frequency: The Power of Personal Vibration*. Hillsboro, OR: Beyond Words, 2009.

Tiller, William A. *Science and Human Transformation: Subtle Energies, Intentionality, and Consciousness*. Walnut Creek, CA: Pavior, 1997.

Wauters, Ambika. *Chakras and Their Archetypes: Uniting Energy Awareness and Spiritual Growth*. Berkeley, CA: Crossing Press, 1997.

Index

About the Author

$\mathcal{D}$anielle Dulsky is a longtime activist for wild woman spirituality and the divine feminine's return. A multimedia artist, yoga teacher and teacher trainer, and energy worker, Danielle is on a mission to inspire women to be fearless creators of their sacred work. She holds the highest designations from Yoga Alliance as an E-RYT 500 and continuing education provider, is the founder of the fully accredited Living Mandala Yoga teacher training programs, and believes in holistic healing for the sensual, creative, and spiritual self. Her work is grounded in holding space for women to harvest their inner Priestess through personally relevant movement alchemy, intuitive artistic practice, and divine feminine spirituality. Danielle leads women circles, Witchcraft workshops, energy healing trainings, and basic and advanced yoga teacher trainings in Phoenixville, Pennsylvania, where she lives with her partner, Ryan, and their two sons. She believes that all women alive today are meant to be instrumental in supporting positive social transformation by enacting their spiritual agency, reclaiming the name Witch as a holy healer, and liberating their inner wild woman.

Website: DanielleDulsky.com
Facebook page: Danielle Dulsky
Instagram: WolfWomanWitch